coffee
NERD

How to Have Your Coffee and Drink It Too

RUTH BROWN

adamsmedia
Avon, Massachusetts

Published by
Adams Media, a division of F+W Media, Inc.
57 Littlefield Street, Avon, MA 02322. U.S.A.
www.adamsmedia.com

ISBN 10: 1-4405-8212-2
ISBN 13: 978-1-4405-8212-7
eISBN 10: 1-4405-8213-0
eISBN 13: 978-1-4405-8213-4

Printed in the United States of America.

10   9   8   7   6   5   4   3   2   1

Library of Congress Cataloging-in-Publication Data
Brown, Ruth,
   Coffee nerd / Ruth Brown.
      pages cm
   Includes index.
   ISBN 978-1-4405-8212-7 (pb) -- ISBN 1-4405-8212-2 (pb) -- ISBN 978-1-4405-8213-4 (ebook)
-- ISBN 1-4405-8213-0 (ebook)
   1. Coffee. I. Title.
   TX415.B765 2015
   641.3'373--dc23

                    2014033051

Always follow safety and commonsense cooking protocol while using kitchen utensils, operat-
ing ovens and stoves, and handling uncooked food. If children are assisting in the preparation
of any recipe, they should always be supervised by an adult.

Illustrations by Eric Andrews.
Cover design by Sylvia McArdle.

This book is available at quantity discounts for bulk purchases.
For information, please call 1-800-289-0963.

Dedication

For James, who prefers
Diet Coke.

Contents

Introduction

When did coffee get so cool?

Just a few years ago, it was something that cost seventy-five cents a cup, existed primarily as a study aid, and came in two varieties—regular or black.

Today, drinks cost upwards of $4, take three times as long to make, and are half as big. Coffee houses have gone from cozy nooks with beat-up old couches and cheap muffins to industrial-chic laboratories where all the customers look like eighteenth-century dandies or really wealthy lumberjacks.

It's easy to write it all off as just another hipster fad, like pickling ramps and bar cornhole leagues. But the truth is that the current trends in coffee—from cheap commodity to totem of cool—have been taking place for decades now, and probably won't be slowing down any time soon. The good news is that most people are just as baffled by the whole thing as you are, so there is still time to get in on the ground floor before all your friends.

Sure, it seems pricey compared to that $1 cup of sludge from your local bodega, but think of it this way: In almost any major city, you can now taste some of the finest coffee in the world, made by top roasters and prepared by award-winning baristas using world-class equipment, without breaking a $10 bill.

And here is the secret: it isn't all that difficult to become an amateur coffee authority. It will cost you far less time and money than your friends who got really into CrossFit or Candy Crush Saga.

How do I know? I am just like you. I am just a regular person who gets out of bed every morning, goes to the office, turns on my computer, goes into the kitchenette and hand-grinds precisely twenty grams of freshly roasted, whole-bean, single-origin coffee and steeps it for four minutes in a full-immersion brewer before going about the rest of my day. I am not a coffee industry professional. I have never been a barista.* I learned about coffee by tasting, testing, experimenting and failing, reading, and talking to people. And you can, too.

Once you've nailed it, your newfound knowledge will spill over into other areas of your life, making you an all-around better and more interesting person.** Picture this: That impossibly hip lady or gent from the bookstore you hang around pretending to browse literary journals in the hope they will be impressed by your apparent knowledge of contemporary Czech short fiction somehow agrees to go on a date with you. You have a couple of hours, $15.25 (there was a quarter under the couch), and a handful of talking points gleaned from half the courses needed for a film studies degree to impress them with. How do you do it? With the greatest coffee date of their life is how.

You start by taking them to a tiny café that is so new and unknown it doesn't even have a Yelp page or a cash register yet. You offer to pay, because you know even the most expensive drink is in your budget. Your knowledge of exotic growing regions (Cariamanga, Sulawesi, Gakenke—where are these places? Don't worry, your date won't know either) will make you sound well-traveled and open up opportunities for casual commentary on current geopolitical issues ("Timor-Leste's coffee industry has really improved in quality since the country gained independence from Indonesia . . .”). Your refined palate ("I'm getting caramel, clove, and a hint of pink gummy bear") suggests you have class and good taste, while your patronage of a local business and friendly repartee with the barista paints you as an engaged citizen and community member.

Most books about coffee are written by industry insiders. This is not one of them. Normal consumers like us neither need nor want to know about the molecular structure of espresso (which is just as well, because I can't explain it)—we just want to know what tastes good.

So consider this book the outsider's guide to becoming a coffee geek. From finding a café to brewing your own drinks, I've filtered out the bullshit and boiled it down to the stuff you actually need to know to get the most out of your cup and not look like a total moron when ordering at coffee shops.

Because now that coffee is cool, there is no reason you can't be, too.

---

* A long time ago—before I knew anything about coffee—I did work in a bar that had an espresso machine, but the less said about that, the better. Suffice to say, the burns have finally healed, and my apologies to anyone who ever ordered fat-free milk—I gave you full cream.

** Results not guaranteed.

Know Your Coffee History

The recorded history of coffee dates back to ancient Ethiopia ... Hey! I can see your eyes glazing over from here. Look, I get it. You picked up this book to learn about what's cool in coffee *now*, so why do we have to talk about long-dead Africans?

Let me put it this way: Imagine trying to learn about punk rock from a fourteen-year-old at the Salt Lake City leg of the Warped Tour. Sure, they can probably give you a pretty thorough rundown of every band currently gracing the front of a Hot Topic T-shirt, but the information will be lacking some fairly important history and context. You need to know about the bands that came *before* punk.

In fact, to really understand the current goings-on in the coffee world, it's important to understand what they *aren't* as much as what they *are*. Just as punk rock was in part a reaction to the polished commercial rock of the 1970s, today's coffee trends are in many ways a reaction to the polished commercial café franchises of the 1990s.

On a more serious note: the coffee trade has a pretty horrible history. It has fueled—and to some extent continues to fuel—slavery, exploitation, poverty, and environmental destruction.

When you buy coffee, you become a part of this system. You don't have to *care* (I mean, you should, you jerk, but you don't *have* to), but you should at least know what you're not caring about.

So bear with me—I'll try to make this as painless as possible. (Or if you really don't care, just skip to the next chapter. It's your book; read it however you want.)

Out of Africa

So how about those ancient Ethiopians? The coffee plant is native to the area, so they had probably been eating and cooking its fruits, seeds, and leaves up in various forms since whichever ancient inhabitant was lucky enough to experience the world's first caffeine buzz and say, "Hey guys, you've *got* to try this. I think it'll really catch on!"

At some point, another canny citizen must have had the inspired idea to roast the bean-shaped seeds inside the fruit, grind them, and boil them with water—and lo, the coffee drink (kinda) as we (sorta) know it today was born.

Out of Africa (Literally This Time)

The next group to catch the coffee craze were the Arabs, which is no great surprise when you consider that Yemen is just a short trip over the sea from the Horn of Africa. More coffee plants were eventually planted there, and by the sixteenth century, the beans had spread throughout much of the Muslim world. At some point, these guys invented the "coffee house," although blueberry scones and poetry slam nights would not appear until many centuries later.

The Turks took a particular liking to the drink, and after the Ottoman Empire took over Yemen in the 1500s, they were also able to wrest control of the region's coffee plantations. They were more than happy to sell coffee beans to other countries, but wanted to keep a monopoly on the actual plants and seeds—a plan that worked until the early seventeenth century, when a wily Dutch merchant managed to smuggle a coffee plant out.

The Dutch subsequently started coffee plantations in their colonies in what are now Indonesia, Sri Lanka, and the southwestern coast of India.

Go West

Throughout the seventeenth century, European traders started to buy these magical beans—originally because they wanted a cut of the increasingly lucrative coffee market in Asia and the Middle East, but eventually bringing both the drink of coffee and the concept of the coffee house to the continent's major cities.

As Europeans developed a taste for this new drink (or, let's be honest, more likely its stimulating effects, because the quality of both the product and its preparation were pretty crappy at the time), some started moving away from the strong, black Turkish style. Instead, they prepared the brew to better suit their palates by filtering out the sediment and adding in milk. Most famously, one of Vienna's first coffee houses, the Blue Bottle, started filtering out the gritty sediment and topping up coffee with milk as early as the 1680s. This smoother-tasting concoction is said to have helped win more people over to the new beverage. (The Austrians would then go on to popularize the idea of topping coffee with whipped cream, and we all know how that turned out . . .)

British colonists also brought the drink with them to American colonies in the seventeenth century, but we'll return there later, because more interesting things were happening elsewhere on the continent.

Coffee Comes to the Americas

Buying up green beans in Asia and reselling them back home became a nice money-spinner for European traders, but naturally, some countries wanted to own the whole supply chain. So in the early eighteenth century, the French and British started creating coffee plantations in *their* colonies—mostly in the Caribbean. In order to man these operations, they did what they had already done with sugar plantations there.

The Portuguese in Brazil also wanted in on this new cash cow, so they pinched some coffee plant seeds from neighboring French Guiana in 1720s (see the "Studs of Coffee History" sidebar for all the sexy details) and started growing their own. Brazil would go on to become the largest coffee-producing country in the world—also on the back of slaves—and the plants eventually made their way to other South and Central American countries. But it wasn't until the nineteenth century that these guys became the big names in coffee production.

Toward the end of the 1700s, what is now Haiti (then the French colony of Saint-Domingue) had become the biggest exporter of coffee in the world. But the slaves working those and other plantations there were living and laboring under *such* horrendous conditions (horrendous even by eighteenth-century slave standards horrendous), they revolted, destroying many of the plantations—not to mention their owners.

This left Ceylon (now Sri Lanka)—under the control of the British—as the new powerhouse. But in the mid-to-late 1800s, a disease called coffee leaf rust laid waste to those plantations, alongside those in India and Indonesia. (The Brits replaced most of their plantations with tea, which is part of the reason they are now a nation of tea drinkers, despite the early popularity of coffee there).

The Latin American countries, now free from their colonial overlords, were there to pick up the slack. (Not that this was necessarily a great blessing for all concerned—in many instances, native peoples were stripped of land, natural environments were destroyed, and plenty of workers were exploited or worse in pursuit of feeding the world's growing appetite for coffee).

STUDS OF COFFEE HISTORY

● ● ●

If all these tales of bean heists and espionage between empires sound thrilling and even a little bit sexy, that's because they totally were (so long as you ignore the parts with the colonialism and the slavery and such). Romantic intrigue, swashbuckling, smuggling—the story of coffee is a regular bodice-ripper. With that in mind, meet two of its studliest rogues:

Gabriel Mathieu de Clieu was an eighteenth-century French naval officer stationed on the Caribbean island of Martinique. In the early 1720s, de Clieu decided it would be a grand idea to cultivate coffee on the island. He knew that King Louis XIV had recently been given a coffee plant by the Dutch, which he was keeping locked up in the royal botanical gardens, so while on leave to Paris, de Clieu set about trying to get his hands on it. According to possibly dubious legend (okay, probably dubious legend, but it's a great story), he successfully talked a French noblewoman into using her feminine wiles to convince a royal physician with access to the gardens to swipe him some cuttings.

De Clieu created a little greenhouse for the plant, and kept it alive during a treacherous voyage that involved a massive storm, a pirate attack, and a jealous shipmate trying to sabotage his plan. But he made it to Martinique in 1723, where he successfully planted the cuttings and helped kick-start France's prosperous coffee plantations in the Caribbean.

Fast-forward a few years. The Portuguese in Brazil were jealously eyeing the French and Dutch plantations—which had now spread down to their neighboring colonies in South America—but neither empire was willing to share. Then in 1727, French Guiana and Dutch Guiana got into a border dispute, and they asked Portugal to mediate. Enter Lt. Col. Francisco de Melo Palheta. This Brazilian Army officer was ostensibly dispatched to French Guiana to resolve the fight, but his real mission was to steal some of their coffee plants. So the story goes, Palheta did this by successfully seducing the wife of the colony's governor. When he was bidding his hosts farewell, she presented him with a bouquet of flowers—with some coffee seeds hidden away inside.

Meanwhile, in Europe . . .

Back in the cultural hubs of eighteenth-century Europe, people were really digging on this new drink. Coffee houses, cafés, kaffeehäuser, and whatever they were called in Amsterdam were multiplying like wet Gremlins. And they weren't just places to drink coffee—they were places to share ideas, see plays, do business, and have a bite to eat. Many of the earlier coffee houses had played up the exotic origins of the drink—à la the giant horse sculptures outside of every P.F. Chang's. In London, some coffee houses displayed stuffed and even live animals like rhinos and elephants. In Paris, the drink became part of a broader craze for all things Turkish in the latter part of the seventeenth century, during which time stylish Parisians were all wearing turbans and robes. But eventually countries developed their own styles and coffee cultures that better reflected local sensibilities: Voltaire and Napoleon played chess at the Café de la Régence in Paris, Alexander Pope and Jonathan Swift discussed literature at Button's Coffeehouse in London, while Casanova went cruising for chicks at Caffè Florian in Venice.

Drinks also continued to move away from their sludgy potboiled provenance (though there was still plenty of that around). Milk, cream, chocolate, or even booze might be added (there is also one account of coffee being mixed with mustard in England, though most of the country spent half of the eighteenth century drunk, so who knows), and the basic idea of immersion brewing—pouring hot water over coffee grounds and leaving it to steep, as opposed to boiling the entire concoction together—gained traction.

In the nineteenth century, more sophisticated brewing devices started to appear in Europe, like the percolator, the siphon brewer, and the drip brewer.

I Want to Drink in America

Across the pond, it was a different scene. America got its first coffee house in the late seventeenth century, but, as good British colonists, folks here were more into drinking tea (and, okay, booze). That is until they decided to stop being such good British colonists and threw all that tea into Boston Harbor (you may have heard about it), and coffee suddenly didn't look so bad after all. The growing Brazilian coffee industry meant Americans didn't need those stinking British, anyway—they could get their own coffee, thank you very much. The Civil War also helped solidify the nation's preference for the drink. Well, parts of the nation. Union soldiers got a ration of beans—usually green—which they could crudely roast, grind, and boil for themselves on the battlefield. The poorer Confederate soldiers weren't so lucky (though, apparently, sometimes they were able to trade some for tobacco with their enemies).

The Yankees may have lagged behind countries like France and Germany when it came to brewing techniques, but they were no slouches when it came to roasting. As technology improved and more commercial roasting operations took off, many Americans stopped buying green beans and charring them at home in favor of pre-roasted coffee from the grocery store. By the late nineteenth and the beginning of the twentieth century, this had become a serious industry, with names like Folgers, Chase

& Sanborn, Arbuckle, Hills Bros., and Maxwell House already appearing on store shelves.

The Century Turns

By this time, Americans had started using pumping percolators, which didn't make amazing coffee, but were certainly a step-up from the previous method of just boiling coffee grounds in water. Of course, back in continental Europe, the Italians had kicked off the century by inventing the espresso machine. The United States answered back by inventing instant coffee. Nice going, America. (Okay, in fairness, quite a few different people in different countries invented early forms of instant, but it was first made commercially successful by an American, then further popularized amongst U.S. troops in World War I).

Fast-forward to the Great Depression. On the downside, the world was mired with horrible economic woes; on the upside, coffee in America was sucking way less. Prohibition had already helped further the popularity of both coffee and the coffee house (I mean, what else were you going to drink?). Better-quality beans were flowing in from Latin America, which the increasingly dominant brand-name roasters were putting into premium labels and blends—though plenty of local grocery stores still sold freshly roasted beans. Vacuum packaging had caught on, allowing beans to be shipped farther and stay fresher. And the coffee market crashed alongside the financial markets, which resulted in low, low prices. Meanwhile, some consumers were finally starting to catch on to superior drip and siphon brewing methods.

But something else was brewing in Europe (or, rather, not brewing)—a little Swiss company you might have heard of called Nestlé was inventing a "better" way of making instant coffee. It dubbed the new product Nescafé, which hit the U.S. market in the late 1930s (where it was later renamed Nescafé Taster's Choice). Oh yeah, and some pretty bad shit was brewing in Germany at the time, too.

When World War II broke out, U.S. forces marched off to war with this newfangled instant coffee in their rations. Things would get worse before they got better.

Further Reading

> *Uncommon Grounds: The History of Coffee and How It Transformed Our World* by Mark Pendergrast is pretty much the gospel on coffee history. The book is especially good for learning about the political, economic, and social impact the coffee trade has had on many Latin American countries (spoiler: a bad one). But it's not all heavy lifting—Pendergrast really brings the U.S. coffee market of the nineteenth and early twentieth centuries to life with his profiles of colorful American coffee barons and their almost comically unscrupulous marketing techniques.

> In 1922, William Ukers, the editor of the *Tea & Coffee Trade Journal*, penned a book called *All about Coffee*, which is now in the public domain and available online at the Project Gutenberg website. If you want to know what coffee nerds were like almost a century ago, Ukers is your man (he actually advocates for a lot of things today's coffee nerds are still trying to popularize: fresh roasting, fresh grinding, manual drip brewing).

TWO

Know Your Coffee Present

Phew! So that's about five centuries out of the way. This brings us to the modern history of coffee in America, which is mercifully only about seventy years—roughly from the end of World War II to today.

Wave Hello

In 2003, a coffee industry professional by the name of Trish Rothgeb, who now co-owns San Francisco's Wrecking Ball Coffee Roasters, published an article in which she introduced the idea of dividing this period of coffee up into three "waves" or movements. The notion took on a life of its own, and the idea of "first-wave," "second-wave," and especially "third-wave" coffee has become well entrenched both inside and outside of the industry.

Like I say, these are movements, not discrete time periods— second-wave and first-wave styles of coffee are still going strong today—but let's look at them chronologically in the periods from which they were born.

First-Wave

When we left off last chapter, American coffee was in a pretty good place, but World War II had just broken out. Let's skip that unpleasantness, and move on to after the war when American coffee got really shitty again. There are a few reasons why.

One is that all those GIs came back with a taste, or at least a tolerance, for instant coffee. Convenience foods were booming generally—and if you were dining on TV dinners and cake mix, why would you take the time to carefully prepare coffee? In the same vein, the coffee vending machine appeared, popularized by the creation of the "coffee break"—a concept basically invented by the coffee industry, by the way, much like the diamond industry invented diamond engagement rings and greeting card companies pretty much invented Secretary's Day.

Meanwhile, the price of coffee beans was skyrocketing, thanks to inflation and plummeting supplies in Brazil. But consumers didn't want to pay more. So the now totally dominant big coffee brands, which were increasingly being bought out by even bigger food conglomerates, started cutting their blends with the cheap and nasty robusta beans (see Chapter 3) they were also using to make instant coffee. And people were brewing these coffees really weak. Basically, the coffee tasted like crap, and a lot of Americans just stopped drinking it.

When coffee people say "first-wave," this is generally what they're talking about—the proliferation of instant coffee and low-quality, mass-produced brand-name beans. This is associated with the period from the end of WWII through the 1960s, but of course, mass-market and instant coffees still line grocery store shelves today.

FIRST SHOTS FIRED

Not everything in that period was dire though. In the late 1940s, an Italian gent by the name of Achilles Gaggia greatly improved upon the original espresso machine, coming up with a way to extract the coffee at a much higher pressure to create what we now consider to be a real "shot" of espresso. In the 1950s, these machines started showing up in Italian cafés in major U.S. cities—most notably New York and San Francisco, where they became popular with local beatniks and bohemians. Today, we would probably consider them hipsters appropriating immigrant culture and *Gawker* would have a field day mocking them, but back then, it was all cool, daddy-o.

The espresso craze, however, wouldn't spread to mainstream America for several more decades, when a different type of Italian-style café took the country by storm. (Spoiler: it rhymes with "schtar schmucks.")

Second-Wave

The second-wave of coffee is synonymous in many people's minds with the rise of that green siren and the onslaught of whipped cream–topped peppermint mochas it wrought. But there is way more to the second-wave than that—Starbucks is just one chapter of the story.

GOOD COFFEE RETURNS

Our story really begins in the 1970s, when more small, independent, high-quality roasters started appearing again. Instead of cans of generic brand-name coffee that had been roasted and ground halfway across the country, some consumers discovered the delights of freshly roasted whole beans, hailing from distinct growing regions or combined deftly into good blends.

So wait, these roasters just showed up out of nowhere overnight? Not so much. There are probably a bunch of very good reasons they appeared when they did, but the simplest way to think of this new wave is within the general rise of the natural and gourmet food movements, especially once the '80s hit. This is the era that crowned stores like Whole Foods and Dean & DeLuca. Yuppies had arrived and they didn't want to eat Wonder Bread anymore—they wanted focaccia.

These folks didn't call themselves or their coffee "second-wave," of course, because the idea didn't exist yet. Instead, they adopted the name "specialty coffee," a term first coined by a coffee importer named Erna Knutsen in 1974, and later adopted by the Specialty Coffee Association of America in 1982. "Specialty coffee" is sometimes used to describe the movement itself, but it's technically a specific grade of beans—those that score at least eighty on the SCAA's 100-point rating system.

From the early renegades in the 1970s, specialty coffee became more ubiquitous through the 1980s and '90s, making its way across the country and eventually into grocery stores—followed by convenience stores, gas stations, airplanes, and even McDonald's. Today, specialty coffee accounts for about 37 percent of the coffee consumed in the United States, according to the SCAA.

IT CAME FROM BERKELEY

Believe it or not, the most important roaster of this era was Peet's Coffee & Tea. Yes, *that* Peet's, like the one at your local mall. But when it opened in 1966, it was a small retail store in the hippie hub of Berkeley, California (just down the road from where Alice Waters would open Chez Panisse—*the* restaurant of the gourmet food movement—a few years later). Here, Alfred Peet, a Dutch immigrant who was born into his father's coffee-roasting business in Holland, used his considerable know-how to source high-quality beans (and teas, presumably, but that is less important here) and extol their virtues to a growing number of devotees. Peet roasted fresh in-store, and he roasted *dark*—a style that caught on with many of his disciples.

These protégés included three friends who wanted to open a roasting business in Seattle. The trio headed down to Berkeley to learn the trade, and in 1971, they set up their own store back in the Emerald City modeled after Peet's. They called it Starbucks.

A NEW BREW

On the brewing side of things, the 1970s saw the rapid rise of the automatic drip-filter coffeemaker. The yellowing Mr. Coffee machine you grew up with might not seem remarkable, but it was a massive step up from the perked coffee most people had been drinking. The popular Melitta manual drip-filter coffeemaker also showed up in the United States around this time (the company had been selling various iterations of the device in its native Germany since 1908).

But as we now know, it was the espresso machine that would eventually come to define this period. Let's head back to Starbucks and fast-forward to the early 1980s. The company now had several stores, but at this point, it was still just a retailer selling whole-bean coffee. But then Starbucks's marketing director, a guy named Howard Schultz, went on a trip to Italy, where he totally flipped for the country's espresso-fueled cafés. He brought the concept home, bought out Starbucks, and reimagined the company in this new vision. Eventually, giant drink sizes, flavored syrups, and the ever-popular Frappuccino made their way onto menus, and the company's popularity exploded. You know what happened next.

Many other specialty roasters and coffee shops got caught up in the chain-store coffee juggernaut themselves—expanding rapidly, bringing in flavored drinks, focusing less on quality and freshness—and a number were actually bought out by Starbucks in the end. But many also stayed true to their original ideals.

ETHICAL CONSIDERATIONS

The second-wave of coffee also coincided with increased awareness amongst both roasters and consumers about where their coffee was actually coming from—and I don't mean "Colombia" or "from a farm."

The 1980s and '90s were rough on all of us—I was wearing Hypercolor overalls, for instance—but they were *particularly* tough on coffee-producing countries. There was the debt crisis and civil war in Latin America, famine in Ethiopia, and genocide in Rwanda, and the Asian financial crisis hit Indonesia hard. Then to make matters worse, wholesale coffee prices plummeted in the late '80s, bottoming out around the mid-'90s, and devastating small coffee farmers and their communities.

At the same time, much of the Western world started waking up to the fact that their sneakers were being made by children in third-world sweatshops. Movements like fair trade, which had been growing since the 1960s, gained more mainstream awareness, while more environmentally focused certifications also appeared.

Many second-wavers—all too aware that the people growing their coffee were having a rough time of it—got enthusiastically on board with these programs. Others were dragged kicking and screaming—after sustained pressure from activists, Starbucks started offering some fair trade coffee in 2000.

IN DEFENSE OF THE CORPORATE COFFEE CHAIN

I felt slightly dirty even typing that, but it is important to understand the massive impact Starbucks and its ilk had on this country—for worse and better. These guys made coffee and coffee houses cool again. Obviously many foodies and granola types were already down with specialty coffee and espresso, but big chain joints made coffee something *teenagers* actually wanted to drink. They introduced espresso and espresso drinks (even if slightly warped variations thereof) to Nowhere, Wyoming. And when some people there discovered those things, they went looking for better versions elsewhere. They got people who'd never paid more than fifty cents for a cup of coffee to shell out $4.

They also helped cement the barista as an important player in the coffee game—the skills of the person preparing your coffee started to become as important as those of the person roasting it. And plenty of people who began their careers wearing a green apron and pushing buttons on semi-automatic espresso machines have gone on to become excellent baristas elsewhere.

All this helped pave the way for the next generation of coffee mavericks, who would take roasting and espresso to new heights.

Third-Wave

Just as the ubiquity of craptastic coffee in the first-wave period drove the pioneers of the specialty movement to shake things up, a new crop of coffee geeks eventually started to push back against the avalanche of coffee-flavored milk shakes flooding the industry.

In the late '90s and early 2000s, while many specialty coffee people were focused on perfecting the pumpkin chai latte, some young guns became more obsessed with perfecting coffee itself—finding the best beans in the world, nailing roasts that highlight their best characteristics, then turning them into a flawless shot of espresso.

This pursuit eventually became a distinct movement *within* specialty coffee—the third-wave—and that has pretty much defined all the trends that are cool in the coffee world right now. Your first step on the road to coffee nerd-dom is familiarizing yourself with the following things.

A WORD ON THE WORDS

● ● ●

Heads up: Most people and companies in the third-wave movement don't actively refer to themselves as "third-wave." It's a bit like the word "hipster"—we all know one when we see one (and deep down, they know who they are—oh, who am I kidding? I wrote a book on nerdy coffee and you're reading it: *we* know who we are), but you rarely hear people actually self-identify as such. Some say "craft coffee," à la craft beer, and others just use "specialty coffee." So just don't go into any coffee shops asking, "Hey, are you guys third-wave?" Okay? Those hipsters will totally side-eye you.

SINGLE ORIGINS AND MICRO-LOTS

If the second-wave introduced roasters and baristas as artisans, the third-wave has done the same thing for the farmer.

The term "single origin" technically just means that the beans all come from one growing region—Java, say, or Kona. That ain't new. But third-wave roasters have hyper-focused on the concept, using beans that only come from small collectives of farms in one area, individual farms, and even specific areas on those individual farms (called a micro-lot).

Where second-wavers might have put "Sulawesi" (an island in Indonesia) on their label, a third-wave roaster will put the region *in* Sulawesi and the name of the actual farm on there, plus a short essay about the farmer, his life story, and the name of his dog on the back. The idea is to capture the unique characteristics of one distinct area, in much the same way that top winemakers do, while highlighting the individual efforts of the people who produced the product.

Further separating out micro-lots has also allowed growers and roasters to reach new heights of quality by singling out the absolute best beans in the absolute best part of a farm. This, again, mimics the practices of the wine industry, where winemakers select grapes from very specific plots of the vineyard for top wines.

On a consumer level, third-wavers argue that single origin coffees help drinkers better understand the distict flavors of different regions and appreciate the individual efforts of coffee farmers. (You might also argue that people just kind of like buying products that have a name, a face, and a story behind them. We've all seen that *Portlandia* scene with the chickens.)

BLENDING IN

Some third-wave cafés and roasters now offer *only* single origins. Others also use blends—a mix of several different beans, usually from different origins—especially for their espresso coffee. Defenders of the blend argue that blending is an art unto itself, allowing them to achieve flavor and aroma profiles that are impossible with one individual origin. Further, many think that single origins just can't stand up to the scrutiny of espresso, which tends to magnify the worst qualities of a bean along with the best—some find the results too unbalanced, or too one-note. The single origin purists counter that this can be overcome with better roasting and preparation techniques.

SOURCING AND DIRECT TRADE

In order to secure those specific beans—and secure the best ones—early third-wave roasters actually started traveling to coffee-growing regions and sourcing their beans directly from farms, instead of working through a labyrinth of third parties from across the ocean. They were far from the first to do this, but they were the first to push it to the forefront of their business models and introduce the idea to consumers.

The thinking behind it (other than probably just wanting to go check out some coffee farms firsthand) is that to get the highest-quality beans, you need to offer the highest prices. By negotiating with farmers and co-ops directly, roasters can offer financial incentives to produce better-quality coffee. If you want to buy a micro-lot, you need to first incentivize a farm to harvest by lot and keep all the beans separate. This is annoying and time-consuming for growers, so there needs to be something extra in it for them.

Another reason is transparency—both for the growers and consumers. The roaster can say to their customers, "Hey, we've *been* there. We know these coffees were grown ethically and sustainably. We know the farmer received a fair price for these beans because we paid it to him ourselves. See? That's his dog's name on the back of the label!"

These relationships became known as "direct trade"—in contrast to fair trade, a system many third-wavers have rejected (more on this in Chapter Six). However, the term has never been regulated in any way, so these days its meaning has become more ambiguous.

Many third-wave roasters today don't actually do literal direct trade coffee. They don't have the time, funds, or sometimes even inclination to spend their lives flying off to far-flung coffee farms, so they work through third parties they trust who are on the ground in those places. But most still try to uphold principles like paying premium and fair prices, sourcing ethically and sustainably, and keeping their supply chain transparent. Or they say they do, anyway.

LIGHTER ROASTS

So if you're putting in all that extra effort and money for coffee from specific origins, you want consumers to actually be able to taste the difference. Ergo, a big trend amongst the third-wave roasters has been increasingly toward lighter and lighter roasts.

The oft-trotted-out metaphor is that of steak: If you buy a really expensive hunk of beef, you don't cook it well-done; you cook it rare or medium-rare so you can still taste all the flavors and juices and the things that *make* it an expensive piece of meat. With coffee, the longer you roast a batch, the less you can taste the unique flavors of the beans and the more you can taste just the flavor of roasting (and eventually the flavor of burning). You'll sometimes hear this called the "Scandinavian style" of roasting, because third-wave roasters there have really pushed the light-roasting envelope, and the moniker has stuck.

Most U.S. roasters don't go quite as light as their Nordic counterparts, but for those used to big, dark roasts, the lighter styles here can still be a little hard to swallow (figuratively, but maybe also literally) at first.

COFFEE AS FRESH PRODUCE

While the second-wave definitely reintroduced more people to the benefits of fresh roasting and grinding, the third-wave has turned this into a gospel. Labeling coffees with the date they were roasted (one roaster I know even includes the time) has become standard practice, and using the beans within a few weeks of that date is *strongly* encouraged (if not outright enforced; some roasters won't sell their product in grocery stores or supply to certain cafés if they don't think they will move it fast enough). This is all part of a broader shift in thinking away from viewing coffee as a commodity item you pick up in a bodega—like a pack of sugar—and more as seasonal, fresh produce, like strawberries.

PREPARATION PERFECTIONISM

So you've spent a bunch of time and money securing an exclusive lot of beans from some hidden gem of a farm halfway across the planet, then roasted them deftly to highlight their best attributes. You aren't about to throw those bad boys into a rusty, old home auto-drip. At a café level, third-wavers are just as purist in their coffee preparation as they are sourcing and roasting.

Making super high quality espresso—both by mastering the technique and using super-expensive, top-of-the-line machines—has always been a feature of most third-wave coffee shops. (To see this passion taken to its most extreme, check out some YouTube clips from the United States Barista Championship. Started by the SCAA in 2002, the high-stakes contest features impeccably groomed young men and women performing fifteen-minute routines in which they make espressos and cappuccinos for a judging panel while gushing about the origin, preparation, and flavor profile of their coffee—all set to music. It's like a TED talk mashed up with *Iron Chef*.) And even batch-brewed coffee became serious business, with many cafés using meticulously prepared French presses instead of automatic filters.

But around the late 2000s, a new obsession emerged for third-wave baristas: manual brewing. That is to say coffee prepared by hand, by the cup, to order. The concept was nothing new—pour-over and siphon brewers had been around in the United States in the kitchens of coffee lovers (and the odd coffee shop) for decades. But many baristas seemed to simultaneously realize: "Huh, those Chemex and Melitta brewers my grandma has are actually pretty cool." Several brewing devices from Japan (where manual brewing has long been an obsession) also started making their way to U.S. shores around this time, which helped further their popularity, because everyone loves weird Japanese gadgets.

It's easy to see why these very hands-on, low-tech methods caught on. They fit nicely with the idea of treating coffee as an artisanal foodstuff and highlighting each bean's unique characteristics. Espresso is a very specific type of coffee drink, and coffee made in large batches an hour ago will never blow your socks off. But manual brew methods allow roasters and coffee shops to showcase the beans at their absolute best, giving the barista maximum control over how the final product tastes. The performance aspect probably doesn't hurt either—while making espresso forces you to stand behind a giant machine well away from the customer, a barista can work their magic with a pour-over or a siphon right on the front counter, putting on a show *and* maintaining conversation the entire time.

Manual brewers have now become fixtures in third-wave cafés, and some places have even eschewed batch-brewing coffee altogether in favor of crafting every cup individually. An even smaller number now don't serve espresso at all. To seal the deal: in 2011, the United States Barista Championship added an equally prestigious Brewers Cup competition to its roster.

EDUCATION

Though not every third-wave coffee business has any interest in schooling the masses on how to grind beans and pour water, educating the public about the difference between good and bad coffee is definitely part of the mission statement for many. Some even do this at a financial loss, offering free or cheap tastings and education sessions in-store, or publishing extensive resources on their websites. For some, it's about spreading the gospel of the third-wave by introducing more people to single origins, processing styles, better brewing methods, and sustainable sourcing. For others, it's more practical—they don't stock sugar or make espresso to go on principal, and they want customers to understand *why* before inciting a minor riot.

Ultimately, consumers who are educated about what goes into producing top-quality coffee are going to be happier paying for it.

NO ARTISANAL FOOD TREND IS AN ISLAND

Just as the first-wave came about during the rise of TV dinners, and the second-wave with sun-dried tomatoes, it is probably no coincidence that the third-wave coffee movement started around the era of the artisan pickle.

A lot of the features of third-wave coffee fit nicely with the current trends in the broader food world toward the small, local, seasonal, and sustainable. Farm-to-table restaurants, menus that read like a laundry list of nearby food producers, farmers' markets, foraging, craft beer: it's all connected, man. And it makes sense: if people are going out to eat organically raised, ethically slaughtered pigs, cooked up nose-to-tail with a side of seasonal vegetables grown on the restaurant's roof, they're not going to stop off at a multinational coffee chain on their way home. (Though ironically, many of the best restaurants still serve absolutely woeful coffee.) This is the age of authenticity and exclusivity, and it's hard to beat a single-origin micro-lot from some remote mountain farm in Bolivia roasted yesterday by a nano-roaster down the street.

NAMES TO KNOW

So just who are these third-wavers, anyway? The three you absolutely, unequivocally, no questions asked, definitely must know are: Counter Culture, which began in Durham, North Carolina, in 1995; Intelligentsia, which was founded in Chicago, also in 1995; and Stumptown, which started in 1999 in Portland, Oregon.

These guys were the most visible pioneers in direct trade relationships, single origins, and trekking the globe to hunt down the best coffees (and often paying famously high prices for them once they did). Stumptown and Intelligentsia have also been super influential in setting trends and very high standards in third-wave cafés around the country, from decor to brewing methods. Of course, these guys are the dinosaurs of the third-wave now (though they all still put out excellent coffee and wield a considerable amount of influence). Younger, smaller, more ambitious roasters and cafés are popping up all the time, pushing new boundaries and creating new trends.

You should find out who pioneered third-wave coffee in your city, too. They were probably taking risks and doing some really cool things while everyone else in town looked at them skeptically and gulped down vanilla chai lattes. I bet they make awesome coffee.

TL;DR

You just skipped past the entire chapter down to this conclusion, didn't you? Fine, but you're only cheating yourself. Here is the entire thing in vastly oversimplified chart form.

WAVE OF PERCOLATION

THIRD-WAVE	SECOND-WAVE	FIRST-WAVE
Super-light roasts	Super-dark roasts	Medium to dark roasts
Direct trade	Fair trade	Commodity trade
Rejecting milk and sugar	Flavored syrup and whipped cream	Nondairy creamer
Cold brew	Frozen coffee beverages	Instant coffee over ice
Single-origin beans	Flavored beans	Crappy beans
Manual pour-over	Espresso	Pumping percolator
Stumptown	Starbucks	Folger's

Further Reading

> *God in a Cup: The Obsessive Quest for the Perfect Coffee* is an excellent firsthand exploration into third-wave coffee during the mid-to-late 2000s by food journalist Michaele Weissman. She profiles the industry leaders at Counter Culture, Stumptown, and Intelligentsia—at a time when all three were arguably at the height of their coolness and influence—and spends a lot of time visiting producers with green-coffee buyers, offering a candid look at both the merits and problems of direct trade coffee.

> *The Blue Bottle Craft of Coffee: Growing, Roasting, and Drinking, with Recipes* (*www.bluebottlecoffee.com*) is a lovely hardback coffee-table book, mostly written from the perspective of Blue Bottle Coffee founder and roaster James Freeman. Though not *quite* as seminal as the big three roasters mentioned here, Blue Bottle had a huge impact on the coffee scene in the San Francisco Bay Area, and is now one of the biggest and best-known names in third-wave. The book has a lot of good practical and educational information on growing, roasting, and brewing, but I think the best stuff is Freeman's story of his own journey into the specialty coffee world as well as his personal philosophies about the bean. It also has recipes for Blue Bottle's outrageously good cookies. I'm not joking; those things are life changing.

> Sprudge (*www.sprudge.com*) started out as a funny coffee gossip blog, but has grown into the best source of third-wave coffee news from around the United States and, increasingly, the world. It is an excellent way to get a handle on the industry's culture and big names, and to hear about all the best new cafés and roasters before your friends do. It also has a

surprisingly thorough section dedicated to cat-related coffee news.

⟩ *Fresh Cup* (*www.freshcup.com*) is a magazine for and about the specialty coffee and tea industry—mostly at a retail level. Some of the content is probably only interesting to professionals (a recent article was subtitled "How to best employ tables, chairs, and more in your café"), but it also often has articles on new trends, techniques, and things happening at the farm level that are interesting to laypeople, too. A lot of its content is free online.

⟩ In a similar vein is *Barista Magazine* (*www.baristamagazine .com*), which is even more inside baseball, but its "field reports" from coffee scenes in other countries offer fascinating insights into how specialty coffee has developed elsewhere on the planet. Recent editions are free online, albeit inexplicably only in a flip-book format.

THREE

Learn What Coffee Is

You know that moment where you're in a restaurant with some-one you don't want to look stupid in front of, and they say, "Oh, you pick the wine," so you look at the menu and realize it's all just a bunch of French and Italian words you don't know? So you just pick one that you can pronounce and afford and try to sound as confident as possible speaking to the waiter. "Tell me about the Timorasso . . . mmm-hmmm . . . uh-huh . . . yeah, that sounds great," you tell them, no matter what they reply. Or you go to some super-nerdy craft beer bar and have to pick between some-thing called Grodziskie and another thing called gruit. Hell, even fancy chocolate shops have become a minefield of Chuao and Porcelanas these days.

So, too, the third-wave coffee shop. It's awesome that, at a café down the road from your apartment, you can now taste fan-tastically well-grown coffees from a tiny family farm in a place you can't even find on a map. But then you ask for a coffee, and the barista replies, "Sure, did you want the Yirgacheffe or the Huehuetenango?" and things don't seem so awesome.

Realistically, the barista will probably happily tell you what those are and what they're going to taste like. But if *you* want to understand for yourself, you just have to learn a little about geography, and how coffee is grown and processed, and many of the answers will be right there. For instance: as long as you know Yirgacheffe is a place in Ethiopia, you know at the very least that it's grown at a high altitude, so it's probably going to have full, bright floral or fruit notes. And once you know that coffees from that region in Ethiopia are typically processed using the washed method, you know it will probably be reasonably acidic and have good clarity. Then once you are actually familiar with the coffee of Yirgacheffe specifically, you know that it is home to unique heirloom varieties boasting a delicate perfume aroma and honeyed sweetness (but don't say it like that out loud).

There are many good reasons to learn about how coffee gets from the ground and into your cup: so you understand what some poor third-world farmer went through for the drink you're only going to consume half of then forget about; so you can chat about the finer points of roasting styles with your favorite barista; or even because you're genuinely curious about the world around you. But if none of those sound compelling, at least read on so you know how to pronounce Huehuetenango (it's "way-way-ten-an-go" and you're welcome) and don't sound like a total n00b when ordering your next cup.

What Even Is Coffee?

If you're the kind of pedant who enjoys smugly reminding people that avocados are actually fruits, peanuts are really legumes, and artichokes are in fact flowers, here is a new factoid for you to annoy your friends with: coffee beans are actually seeds. They *look* kind of like beans—presumably where the name comes

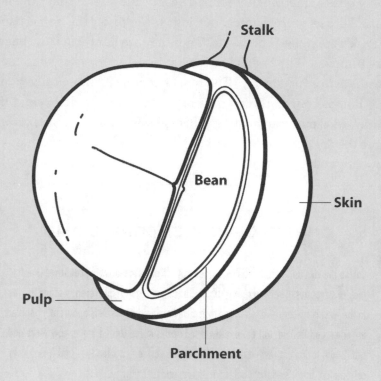

Stalk

Bean

Skin

Pulp

Parchment

Inside a coffee "cherry."

from—but they are really the seeds of the fruit of the coffee tree—which is referred to as a "cherry" but is in fact a type of berry. Yes, everything is a lie.

In a nutshell, the life story of a coffee bean from farm to your belly goes something like this: The "cherries" (and that's the last time I'll use scare quotes, but just so we're on the same page) grow on small trees or plants. Once they are harvested, the beans are removed. The beans are then shipped to roasters, who toast them up to a nice brown. The roasters then sell them on to you.

But, of course, the entire story is far more complex, and the variables at every level of the process—where the beans are grown, how they're processed, and how they're roasted, just to name a few—ultimately dictate how awesome or terrible a cup will be.

CH-CH-CH-CH-CHERRY BOMB

Coffee cherries don't tend to be consumed outside of coffee-growing countries (I'm told they're sweet but usually unremarkable). But something that has recently made its way to the West is cascara—a tea *made* from dried coffee cherries. It is apparently popular in Yemen and Bolivia, but quite a few trendy cafés in the United States now serve and sell it, too. It doesn't taste anything like regular coffee—it's fruity—and it isn't very caffeinated, but it's educational, sustainable, and pretty tasty.

Plant Identification

There are a bunch of different species and varieties in the Coffea genus of plants, but only two you need to care about. The vast majority of the world's coffee comes from the Coffea arabica plant, which is a good thing because it yields the best coffee beans. The rest is almost entirely from the Coffea robusta plant, which yields shitty coffee beans that are bitter and dull.

So why is anyone even growing or selling robusta at all? For a start, as the name suggests, it's more robust. It is disease resistant, can grow at lower altitudes than arabica, and has a higher yield. To put it another way: it is way cheaper. It is no coincidence that at times of high coffee prices and bad economies, more robusta has historically found its way into coffee blends. It has also long been a staple ingredient of instant coffee, presumably because instant coffee tastes like crap anyway, so why waste the extra money on better beans?

Another reason robusta persists is that it tends to give espresso coffee more crema—that is the thin golden froth that occurs on top of the coffee. Italian espresso lovers are mad for crema. So some Italian espresso blends incorporate robusta for that reason (I'm sure its price doesn't hurt either), though many roasters believe it's not worth the tradeoff.

Of course, plenty of arabica coffee still sucks, either because it is grown or processed badly. But robusta mostly just sucks no matter what you do with it.

Arabica Nights

If you thought you just got away with learning only about two plants: hell no. Arabica comes in a bunch of different varieties, all of which have their own unique characteristics. Here are just a few worth knowing:

> **Typica:** This is *the* original coffee variety the Europeans planted all over the world, from which most other coffee varieties have spawned. It is basically The Yardbirds of coffee varietals, the breeding ground for caffeine's Eric Clapton, Jeff Beck, and Jimmy Page.

> **Bourbon:** The French planted some typica on the island of Bourbon (now Réunion; it's near Madagascar) in the early eighteenth century. Eventually, it mutated into its own variety, one with higher yields and often a slightly sweeter flavor. Bourbon (pronounced "burr-bone," not like the liquor) also went on to sow its wild oats throughout the world, and also has many offspring varieties.

> **Pacamara:** Here is an example of a really incestuous one. It is a hybrid between pacas—a natural Bourbon mutation from El Salvador—and maragogype—a natural typica mutation from Brazil, known primarily for its big beans. So its mom is its dad's aunt, is what I'm saying.

> **Ethiopian heirloom varieties:** Remember how Europeans took some typica from Yemen and basically littered the world with its offspring, all mutating and procreating together (not unlike European nobility, which is pretty funny because almost all of the world's plantations were fathered by a single coffee plant owned by Louis XIV)? But remember how coffee was already growing natively in Ethiopia? So Ethiopia still has thousands of indigenous varieties that didn't spawn from those typica plants. Unfortunately, less is known about these varieties on a botanical level, so they tend to be more broadly classified by the area they grow in, such as Harar, Sidama, and our old pal Yirgacheffe.

> **Gesha:** Gesha (or sometimes geisha) is believed to distantly hail from Ethiopia, but these days, it is grown in Central and South America—most notably in Panama. It is well known for being some of the most crazy expensive coffee on the market (some really good green gesha beans famously went for $170 a pound in 2010), due to its scarcity and unique, highly desirable floral sweetness and aroma.

> **SL-28 and SL-34:** Sometimes varieties don't mutate naturally —sometimes they are made in a lab. Kenya is big into lab-made varieties, most famous of which are SL-28 and SL-34— created by a company called Scott Laboratories. SL-28 has drought-resistant properties, while SL-34 thrives in heavy rainfall. Both are prized for their juicy, fruity flavors, and complex acidity. SL-28, which is generally considered the superior of the two, is particularly known for its distinctive black currant flavor.

> **Timor Hybrid:** In the nineteenth century, leaf rust started killing off much of the Netherlands's coffee plantations in Indonesia. So they replaced loads of it with robusta, and the Dutch, presumably, had to learn to force down really crappy coffee. Eventually, some arabica and robusta plants on the island of Timor shacked up together, creating a natural hybrid of the two. This hybrid has robusta's disease resistance, but sadly also much of its suckiness. Still, because it is part-arabica, it can crossbreed with other arabicas, and has since been used in a number of other hybrids, watering down the suckiness a little while retaining some of its disease-resistant superpowers. It is basically that embarrassing ancestor no one likes to admit to having.

Grow and Behold

So now we know that coffee variety matters. But what also matters is *where* those coffee varieties are grown. Much like wine, coffees from different places have a different "terroir"—a pretentious word that basically refers to the distinctive characteristics that an area's soil, climate, and geography impart to the things that grow there. A Chardonnay from Burgundy tastes very different from a Chardonnay from California, and Bourbon grown in Rwanda tastes different from Bourbon from El Salvador. And New Yorkers will tell you that a bagel made in New York tastes different from one made anywhere else, though that one is probably bullshit.

Coffee plants can probably be grown anywhere that has sun, some rain, and no frost. But, also like wine grapes, you can only make *good* coffee from plants grown in specific regions. There are vineyards in South Dakota—doesn't mean there should be. The best coffee regions all lie in what's known as the "bean belt," which is roughly between the Tropic of Cancer and the Tropic of Capricorn (if you can mentally conjure up Baja California, Mexico, down to São Paulo, Brazil, that's the gist), and at higher altitudes—from around 3,000 feet to 6,000 feet and above.

The Air Up There

Even within that 3,000 feet to 6,000 feet range, the elevation a coffee is grown at can have a big impact. For the most part, coffee plants grown at low altitudes (and in the context of high-quality coffee, 3,000 feet is low altitude) are slackers. They lie about in the sun all day, ripen quickly, and go soft (literally). They don't

Latin America Africa Asia

The "bean belt."

have to work hard, so they don't, and as a result, their flavors tend to be milder and duller. They're burned-out trust-fund kids—all potential and no follow-through.

High-altitude coffees are survivors. They're stuck freezing their butts off on the top of some mountain, enduring periods of intense heat and intense sunlight. Fewer coffee cherries make it up there, but the ones that do are the hard-asses, and all their hustling and bootstrapping pays off in brighter, fruitier flavors. There are exceptions, for sure—there are some nice lower-altitude Brazilians, for instance. And hey, sometimes you *want* to chill out with an earthy, mellow low-altitude coffee. But as a rule, the higher the altitude, the more highly prized the bean.

Seasons of Love

Although you can buy some sort of coffee year-round, the plant itself is as seasonal as blueberries or professional hockey. Because it is grown all over the world, *something* is almost always in season—Brazilian farmers might be harvesting in May, while Hawaiian farmers might not start until October—but specific regions will only be available to buy at specific times of the year.

As you're about to learn, there is a necessarily long time between picking coffee cherries and the beans actually arriving at a roaster—it's not like the kale that shows up at a farmers' market a day after being picked. So a coffee that is "in season" at your local coffee shop was actually picked months ago. Supplies of those beans will last only a limited time; then the roaster will move on to the next region in season.

Not-So-Easy Pickings

Next time you gripe about paying $14 for a 10-ounce bag of coffee, spare a thought for the folks who actually had to pick that coffee—the people at the bottom of the coffee-production food chain. Let's say there are about 2,600 beans in that bag. That is 1,300 coffee cherries. Every one of those coffee cherries had to be picked by hand, which means long hours of backbreaking work outdoors. The best farms are very persnickety about only picking the best cherries at their peak, and coffee cherries ripen at uneven intervals, so pickers have to return to the same trees again and again looking for ripe cherries. A lot of the time, they are paid only for the cherries they collect, not by salary or by the hour.

It's a Process

Getting the coffee beans out of the coffee cherries might sound like a relatively simple task, but it's actually much more involved than just taking a bite and spitting out the seed (I mean, you could do it this way, but the results wouldn't be great). Once they've been picked, the beans have to spend a bit more time being "processed" before they're ready for the roaster. There are several different ways this can be done, and the method chosen will have a significant effect on the final taste of the coffee.

DRY PROCESSING
Also called natural processing, this is the oldest and simplest method. In this practice, the cherries are picked, cleaned, and then left out on mats or patios to dry in the sun for several

weeks. Once the cherry has shriveled up, a machine strips the desiccated fruit part away.

The long drying process imparts a lot of sweetness and berry flavors to the bean, and these coffees are often described as tasting wild or exotic. But "wild" can be a bad thing, too—it's a difficult process to control, and there is always a risk that the cherry will ferment or go bad.

WASHED PROCESSING

For growing regions that can spare the water (and many can't), this method—also called wet processing—has become more popular and preferred by many growers and roasters. After the cherries are picked, they are "pulped" by machine, stripping them of all but a thin layer of pulp around the bean, which sports the highly unappetizing name of "mucilage."

Then, one of two things happens. Traditionally, they are put into a tank of water to ferment for anywhere from a few hours to a few days, during which time the mucilage comes off. But now some people are instead using a machine called a "demucilager," which scrubs and washes away the mucilage. After the beans emerge from one of these two treatments, they are dried either in the sun or by machine.

Washed coffees typically have higher acidity, lighter bodies, and cleaner flavors than their dry-processed counterparts.

PULPED NATURAL PROCESS

Also known as semi-washed, honey processed, or semi-lavado (don't bother trying to look that one up online because Google is *convinced* you mean Demi Lovato), this is kind of a mash-up of washed and dry processing. It starts out like the former—the cherries are picked and then pulped—then switches to the latter—the beans, with the mucilage still on them, are dried in the sun. The characteristics of these coffees are also somewhere between the two—they typically have the cleanliness of the washed with the sweetness of the dry.

WET HULLING

Many (but not all) Indonesian coffees are processed with a unique method called "wet hulling" (or *Giling Basah* in Bahasa Indonesia). This starts out like your washed process, with the cherries being pulped (which removes the skin), fermented (which removes the mucilage), and set out to dry. But the beans don't get to rest long. Partway through, their leisurely sun-baking is interrupted so that their parchment layer can be removed by machine. After this, they go back to drying—but they've changed, man.

At its best, wet hulling gives the coffee an earthy, foresty quality; at worst, it becomes musty and kind of funky. Even done well, the resulting flavors aren't everyone's cup of tea.

KOPI LUWAK

Wait, isn't there some type of coffee that's pooped out by wild catlike animals? Pretty much—it's called kopi luwak, and it is the result of civets in Indonesia and the Philippines eating coffee cherries and pooping out the beans. Once upon a time, this was just something wild civets did in that part of the world, so locals would pick up the coffee beans and use them. But at some point, foreigners caught on to the phenomenon, and word of the "exotic" processing "technique" spread, the line being that civets only select the best, ripest berries and the acids in their stomachs give the bean a unique flavor. Suddenly, there was a global market for this stuff. The scarcity of the beans themselves commanded crazy-high prices, and viral news stories about how "cat poo coffee costs $30 a cup!" plus a mention on *Oprah* drove demand even higher.

Here is the real deal with kopi luwak: Most specialty coffee professionals agree that it is just not very good quality coffee. If that isn't enough to turn you off, much of it comes from farms that lock civets in tiny cages and feed them nothing but coffee cherries because there simply isn't very much "wild" kopi luwak around. And much of what is labeled as "kopi luwak" is believed to be counterfeit—the industry has very little oversight.

Known Origin

But let's back up here a little. Where are all these coffee-growing regions, anyway, and what do their coffees taste like? I wish I could tell you definitively "Colombian coffees taste like this, and Indonesian coffees taste like *this*." But you already know that coffees vary significantly by varietal, processing method, and altitude. Equally, coffees grown in different parts of different countries taste, well, different.

Think of Indonesia (or pull up Google Maps here if you can't; it's only the 4th most populous country on Earth): It's basically a bunch of islands spread out at the bottom of Asia. You've got coffees grown in the north of Sumatra, then coffees grown on Sulawesi. Those islands are separated by about 1,800 miles and much of Malaysia. Meanwhile, Mexico and Guatemala basically grow coffee across the border from each other, but we don't lump those together.

That is all just a giant caveat to say that the following are some sweeping generalizations about coffees from particular regions—and the kind of aromas and flavors you can roughly expect to find in those coffees—but you will come across plenty of exceptions. And this is by no means a definitive list of coffee-growing regions, either—some of the world's largest producers, like Vietnam and India, are missing. Rather, what follows are the origins you're most likely to find lining third-wave coffee shops' repurposed barn-wood shelves at the moment.

SOUTH AMERICA

When you think South American coffee, think of the Andes. Much of the coffee from Colombia, Peru, and Bolivia is grown along the mountain range, making for some of the highest-altitude coffees in the world—some farms in Bolivia are more than 8,000 feet above sea level. Typically washed, these coffees tend to be quite sweet, with gentle acidity and medium body. You may also smell and taste hints of nuts, honey, caramel, vanilla, and molasses.

The exception here is Brazil, which is a pretty dang big exception, because it's the largest producer in the world (though a lot of what it makes is for cheap and mass-produced). Unlike with its neighbors, Brazilian coffee is generally grown at lower altitudes and is typically dry or pulped-natural processed, so they tend to be lower in acidity and clarity. They're mild, sweet, and chocolaty, and are often used in espresso blends for these qualities.

CENTRAL AMERICA

When human beings eventually become entirely sedentary, couch-based life forms that interact only via Snapchat and consume all food in pill form, the coffee pills will probably taste something like a Central American coffee. Thanks to the region's proximity to the United States, these are what most Americans think of when they think of a typical "coffee" flavor. Which is not to say they're generic or unremarkable—far from it. Guatemala, Panama, El Salvador, and Costa Rica produce some of the finest coffee around, and Honduras, Nicaragua, and Mexico (which, yes, is in North America, *I know*, but its coffee, grown at the bottom of the country, may as well be Central) also produce some very fine stuff.

Grown at high altitude and usually washed, Central American coffees often taste like a fruit and nut chocolate bar—very well balanced, light to medium bodied, with fruity sweetness and bright acidity.

One notable exception is the aforementioned gesha variety—the current darling of the coffee world, which is most famously grown in Panama but is now spreading all over the continent. Intense, complex, and rich with floral sweetness, these guys crush the prestigious Best of Panama contest every year and command hefty price tags in return, but are quite different from most other varieties grown in the region.

When drinking Central American coffees, you might pick up on notes of chocolate, nuts, caramel, vanilla, and citrus. With gesha, expect flowers, perfume, honey, tropical fruit, citrus, and berries.

NORTH AMERICA

Like Christmas decorations and American flags, coffee is something the United States is *capable* of producing domestically, but it's rare to actually see the homegrown stuff for sale on shelves. Hawaii is the only part of the country where you can grow decent coffee—and only certain parts of Hawaii—so only a relatively small amount is produced. And those growers have to pay first-world prices and wages to produce it. As a result, Hawaiian coffee is really pricey, even for top U.S. roasters—many of whom don't think it's worth the extra cash. I include it here, however, because hey, it's gosh darn American coffee, and you can buy online directly from roasters in the Aloha State, if you're feeling flush. (You will often see coffees labeled "Kona Blend" or "Kona Style" on grocery store shelves, but these are a con, usually containing about ten percent Hawaiian coffee and 90 percent from elsewhere).

Coffee is grown on several of Hawaii's islands, all of which have their own profiles and use different processing methods. But the most famous is Kona, which tends to produce coffees that are medium bodied, floral, fruity, and sometimes quite acidic even though the coffee there is grown at a relatively low altitude.

Things you might taste and smell include berries, citrus fruits, tropical fruits, flowers, vanilla, and wine.

ASIA

The majority of Asia's coffee comes from Vietnam and India and sucks so bad you've probably never even heard of Vietnamese or Indian coffee (though perhaps you will eventually; both are apparently starting to produce some less sucky stuff now).

In the specialty coffee world, you're only going to get the goods from Indonesia, Papua New Guinea, and sometimes East Timor. We've already talked about Indonesia's wet-hulling process—which gives coffees an earthy or musty quality and is sometimes even likened to the smell of weed (so basically, not unlike your friends after they return from backpacking through Indonesia)—but not all Indonesian coffee is made that way, nor is Timor's or PNG's. These are usually processed via a washed or pulped natural method, and range from spicy and aromatic to sweet and fruity, with the kind of flavors Westerners tend to think of as "exotic."

With Indonesian coffees, you might taste and smell herbs, cinnamon, tobacco, leather, wood, and bittersweet chocolate, while New Guinean coffees can offer up tropical fruit, citrus, vanilla, and floral notes.

AFRICA

Ethiopia is to coffee as the United States is to Olympic basketball. Sure other countries have one or two star players, but basketball was born in America and coffee was born in Ethiopia. Where other coffee-growing countries are dealing with a handful of plant varieties and maybe a century or two of growing, Ethiopia is home to thousands of native varieties and thousands of years of cultivation. As a result, generalizing about Ethiopian coffees is like generalizing about the playing style of the entire NBA. But hey, let's give it a go! Roughly, we can divide the country's coffees up by the two dominant processing styles. Dry-processed Ethiopians, like those in the eastern region of Harar, often pack a wild, fruity flavor and sweetness, frequently likened to blueberries or wine. Washed Ethiopians—common in the Sidama region, and its famed subregion of Yirgacheffe—tend to be lighter-bodied and, especially in Yirgacheffe, are defined by intense floral aromas and citric acidity.

Down in Kenya, processing is a big deal. The country has its own twist on washed processing, which involves two fermentations, followed by soaking the beans in water. Add that to the aforementioned SL-28 and SL-34 varieties, which make up a lot of Kenya's coffee, and you get a cup that is typically intensely acidic but also sweet and fruity, often with the varietals' signature black currant flavor.

Coffees from Burundi and Rwanda tend to be similar to Kenyans, albeit slightly more muted, and sometimes a little floral and Ethiopian-esque.

SOLO CUP

Like packs of disposable razors from the grocery store, coffee beans usually come two-for-one in each coffee cherry. But sometimes—maybe five percent of the time—the beans mutate, and you get a single, more round-shaped bean instead. These are known as "peaberries" (or *caracol* in Spanish, which means "snail"). Producers from various regions will sometimes separate out these beans, and sell them as a distinct product (often with a distinctly higher price tag to match). But perhaps nowhere does this quite so prolifically as Tanzania—to the point where "Tanzanian coffee" and "peaberry coffee" are basically synonymous in many people's minds. Are they actually that different from regular Tanzanian coffees (which are roughly akin to those of Burundi and Rwanda)? Some think they're more complex, maybe a little brighter, some don't. Either way, there is nothing mind-blowingly special about them, no. Producers often sort the peaberries out from their regular harvests anyway because their unique size and shape means they roast differently than regular beans.

Milling Around

Now we've completed our brief world tour of where all this is taking place, let's get back to the production process.

The beans have finished all the processing that will take place at the farm level (this stage is called "wet milling," by the way, but between wet processing and wet hulling, this is a monumentally unhelpful term. The next stage, you will be shocked to learn, is called "dry milling.") After this, the beans are usually left to chill out in storage for a month or so to strengthen up and get their moisture levels right so they can withstand travel and roasting. At this point, the beans still have a thin layer of "parchment" around them, so once they're done resting, they get sent off to a mill to have it removed. Now stripped naked and bare, they become what is known as "green coffee" or "green beans" (and they are, in fact, usually the color green at this stage, though sometimes a bit more blue or gray). They are then sorted either by hand or machine for size and density, and the defective beans—wrong size, wrong color, eaten by bugs—are tossed out. Now the beans are ready to be roasted.

Shipshape

Of course, before that can happen, the beans have to actually *get* to a roaster. Overnight FedEx is not an option. Shipping coffee involves weeks or months spent in ports and on boats before the beans even hit the United States, then more travel over land before they finally reach a warehouse and eventually your favorite local roaster. While not something you as a consumer have to worry about that much, this entire process is a gamble because the beans can be damaged or ruined by delays, heat, humidity, or poor storage conditions.

CUTTING THE CAFFEINE

🫘 🫘 🫘

Until scientists work out how to grow good caffeine-free coffee beans, making decaf coffee means the caffeine has to be removed *after* the beans have been processed (but typically before they actually reach the roaster). There are quite a few ways to do this, some of which involve chemicals, but most good roasters opt for more environmentally friendly water-based processes.

Very (*very*) roughly: You can extract caffeine by soaking green beans in water, but that also tends to soak out most of the flavor and oils. These methods turn that problem into a solution by soaking each batch of green beans in the very water the previous batch had used, but with the caffeine filtered out. That way, the beans are immersed in their natural oils while the caffeine is removed, and less flavor is lost.

If that made zero sense to you: a Canadian outfit inexplicably named Swiss Water Decaffeinated Coffee Company, which is responsible for decaffeinating a lot of America's specialty coffee, has a very good animated video on its website (*www .swisswater.com*) that explains the whole thing much better than I can with words.

Production Roast

Let's assume our beans didn't get lost or destroyed somewhere between Rwanda, the Port of San Francisco, and your hometown. Once they arrive, the roasters will roast a small sample of the beans and cup them (see Chapter 4, Coffee Cuppings), to make sure they're not borked and to decide the best way to roast that particular lot—which flavors and aromas to highlight, which to downplay. This is important to know because two roasters can interpret the same beans in different ways (and, in fact, if you live in a city where multiple roasters use the same coffee brokers, sometimes several different roasting outfits will be using the same kind of beans at once—which probably annoys them, but is fun for coffee nerds).

Think of it like the Batman movies—there's campy Adam West Batman, wooden Val Kilmer Batman, broody Michael Keaton Batman, and even broodier Christian Bale Batman (and also George Clooney Batman, but the less said about that the better). It's all the same source material, but the writers, actors, and directors choose what *kind* of Batman they want to bring to the screen. Do you want to bring out this coffee's brighter, simpler Adam West notes, or its more deep and complex Christian Bale side? And how are you going to do that?

Real Roasting for Real This Time

Once the roasting style is decided, it's time to get cooking—literally. Many people think of the coffee beans they buy as a basic staple like sugar or flour, which has been through some industrial level processing, but is basically uncooked. That is true for the green beans the roasters receive, but by the time the beans hit the shelves of your local coffee shop, they have been prepared with as much skill and artistry, if not more, as the small-batch cookies and artisan doughnuts they sell from the same counter.

There are a few different types of coffee-roasting machines, but just about every third-wave roaster you'll come across will use a drum roaster, so let's not waste time on the others (although if you ever get the chance to watch a hot-air or fluid-bed roaster in action, go for it—seeing the beans fly around a see-through container like one of those money-blowing machines is fun). These machines come in all shapes and sizes, and can be heated by anything from a wood fire to gas, but their defining feature is a rotating cylindrical metal drum that tumbles the beans around while they roast inside, a bit like a clothes drier.

Most of these drum roasters are pretty low-tech—they've worked fundamentally the same way for about a century, and many third-wave roasters use vintage models anyway (though possibly for aesthetic and economic reasons more than anything else). Sure, there are some newfangled tools and gadgets that help, but the fate of the beans is still pretty much in the hands of the user. Good roasters work these machines like a fine pâtissier—there is a basic recipe to follow, but they also have to use their own sense of smell, sight, and gut instinct to decide when to alter the temperature or air flow or stop the roast altogether so that they achieve the exact flavors and aromas they're seeking.

Here is a basic rundown of what goes on:

BEANS GO IN

The roaster weighs the right amount of beans, then loads them into the roaster.

THINGS START TO HEAT UP

As the beans get hotter, the moisture inside them escapes and evaporates. The beans start to turn yellow or orange, and then a light brown. At this stage, they are absorbing a lot of heat, but they can only handle so much . . .

THE SWEET SCIENCE

The beans start to expand, and get even browner. The starchy carbohydrates inside are turning into sugar and caramelizing.

A CRACKING START

Bam! That's not the Batman thing again; when the temperature inside the roaster gets high enough, the beans start to release all that built-up heat, making an audible popping sound. This is known as "first crack."

CRACKING ON

As the first crack continues, the beans get browner, larger, and less dense. When the first crack is done, the beans will once again start to take on heat, eventually leading up to a second release and crack.

HAVE ANOTHER CRACK

As the second crack hits, the beans are getting quite dark, their oils are starting to come to the surface, and the distinct "character" of the bean starts to disappear behind the flavor and

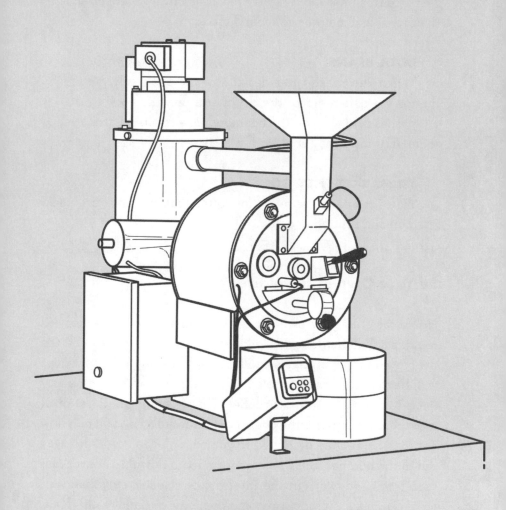

A drum roaster.

aroma of, well, roasted coffee. More traditional roasters may go well into this phase, but lighter-roasting third-wavers often stop their roast well before the second crack.

COOL BEANS

When the roaster decides the beans are ready, he or she dumps the coffee out of the drum and into the cooling tray. A fan passes cold air over the beans, while a spinning arm sweeps them around so they cool evenly.

TO MARKET THEY GO

Now the beans are ready for coffee making. They are packaged up and sent off to cafés and stores .

Be Your Own Roast Master

Home roasting is its own special subgenre of coffee nerdery (if regular coffee nerds were Trekkies, homeroasters would be the people who write Star Trek fan fiction), and something that goes well beyond the scope of this book. Suffice to say, it is in no way necessary to roast your own coffee. Thanks to the proliferation of great roasters around the country and the Internet, you can now get top-shelf coffee delivered to your door, even if you live way out in the boonies. But if you do want to go down this particular rabbit hole, anyway—in the interests of science, sustainability, saving money, making awesome birthday gifts (it really does), or because your house just doesn't smell enough like a forest fire, then it isn't hard to get started. Some cities have stores that sell green coffee beans, but many people buy online at

Sweet Maria's (*www.sweetmarias.com/store*) or Roastmasters (*www.roastmasters.com*), both of which also sell home-roasting equipment.

Dedicated home machines start from around $110 for a little entry-level air roaster through to $1,250 for a fancy drum roaster, but you actually don't need those if you're just interested in trying your hand at roasting for fun or curiosity. You can roast coffee in a home popcorn maker—both the stovetop Whirley Pop and most electric air poppers—and even just in the oven. Here is a fairly crude method if you just want to try it out:

GAS OVEN ROASTING

Yeah, it has to be a gas oven. You'll also need a small amount of green beans (one pound typically costs between $5 and $10), a perforated baking pan (those are the ones with small holes in them; if you don't have one, a kitchenware store or your great aunt will), and a metal colander. You might also want to crack open a window or ten for this—there will be smoke.

1. Preheat the oven to 500°F (or 450°F if it is a convection oven).

2. Spread a single layer of beans across the pan (only the perforated part of it).

3. When the oven is ready, place the pan onto the middle shelf.

4. You should start to hear the first crack somewhere around seven minutes (maybe more in a convection oven), and you should be able to see that the beans are turning brown.

5. Wait at least a couple more minutes, then either take the tray out (use oven mitts!) or wait a few more minutes until the beans are *almost* at the color you desire (they will continue to roast for a bit after you take them out, so don't wait too long).

6. Dump the beans into your colander. Stand over a sink or go outdoors, and shake them around. This will cool them down and get rid of the chaff (the little bits of parchment that didn't get removed at the mill), which can get pretty messy. The faster you can cool your beans off, the better.

Further Reading

> Stoneworks (*http://auction.stoneworks.com*) is an online auction platform where some of the finest green beans in the world are traded. You can view past auction results to get an idea of the kind of prices premium lots sell for, and the kind of roasters who pay for them. It's more fascinating than it sounds, I promise.

> Counter Culture Coffee (*www.counterculturecoffee.com*) has an excellent interactive graph on its site that shows the relationships between different coffee varieties. It will probably send you down an hours-long rabbit hole of Googling obscure strains, but it is a great visual guide to all the different plants and their messed-up family trees.

> Roaster maker Probat Burns (*www.probatburns.com*) has a fun little toy on its website that lets you see what goes on inside a drum roaster. You can add beans and play around with the air pressure, heat type, and temperature to get an idea for what roasters (both the machines and the people) actually do. It's a bit like something you'd find at a children's

science museum, but surprisingly instructive. You can find it by searching for their "Spotlight on Drum Roasting" article.

> As previously mentioned, Sweet Maria's is pretty much the one-stop shop for all things home roasting. In addition to selling green beans and roasting equipment, it has advice, resources, and forums for roasting nerds.

> *Home Coffee Roasting: Romance & Revival* by Kenneth Davids, who has written several other very good books about coffee that are also worth checking out, is pretty much what it says on the label. It is a great primer on the history and science of roasting, and also contains detailed guides to many different home-roasting methods.

> *Roast Magazine* (*www.roastmagazine.com*) is a trade magazine for roasters, but it reports on a lot of interesting issues and stuff happening at the farm level and in various coffee-growing regions. I'm not saying you should subscribe (unless you're looking to get into home roasting, maybe), but definitely leaf through a copy if you ever see it around.

FOUR

Find Your Coffee Shop

If your current knowledge of coffee starts with Folgers Crystals and ends with twenty-ounce sugar-free caramel lattes, you could be forgiven for wanting to steer clear of hoity-toity third-wave coffeehouses until you've done a little more practice and research at home. But as intimidating as they may be, cafés are the best place to get your feet wet in the world of coffee geekery. In fact, you don't want to just dip your toes in the water—you need to jump all in like it's the first day of summer break.

Cafés have a lot more to offer than just overpriced scones and sketchy Wi-Fi. Find the right kind of place, and you can sample amazing coffees you've never heard of, try out new and exotic brewing styles, and meet baristas who actually want to school you in the ways of the beans. If you get chummy and ask nicely, you might even get to see the roasting process, attend coffee tastings, and learn about the latest caffeinated goings-on in your city.

Many people start their exploration of quality coffee by buying a brewer and some beans and trying to muddle their way through it at home. This is backward—imagine trying to learn how to play basketball from a book without ever having seen a real game. So coffee shops are where your education should begin, because you need to learn what good coffee tastes like before you can make it yourself. When it does come time to make it yourself, you will already know a bunch of professionals to help guide you on your path.

So before you even buy your first bag of beans, you need to rack up some hours on the bench—probably a communal one fashioned out of repurposed old-growth timber, next to a free-lance graphic designer blasting dubstep out of his massive head-phones, but a bench nonetheless.

Finding the Right Kind of Coffee Shop

There are a lot of stereotypes about third-wave coffee shops: young, intimidatingly hip baristas sporting designer cycling caps, knuckle tattoos, and elaborately groomed facial hair; fixed-gear bikes chained up out the front and possibly moonlighting as decor on the walls; obscure indie band B-sides playing on a vintage stereo. And most of those stereotypes are pretty accurate. The latest movement in coffee is still pretty new, and is still over-whelmingly populated by people who look the same, dress the same, and decorate their cafés the same way. This is bad news for diversity—and there is probably a very good post-doctoral thesis to be written on the intersectionality of race, class, gender, and the specialty coffee industry—but it sure does make finding good cafés easier.

That's not to say that there aren't good coffee shops out there that break the mold. Just that you can seek out those when you have a better idea of what you're actually looking for when it comes to coffee. For now, be on the lookout for waxed mustaches and bespoke trucker caps.

This situation won't last forever. Starbucks has already set up a couple of covert storefronts in Seattle designed like trendy independent coffee bars, and in the coming years, we're definitely going to see more venues that ape high-end coffee shops without actually serving high-end coffee (or without serving it well, anyhow). But right now, if a café *looks* like your vision of the clichéd hipster coffee shop, then it probably is one.

How to Find a Good Coffee Shop

So, what if you don't know what a cool coffee shop looks like to begin with? Consult this simple checklist for things to look for, and things to avoid.

GO ON IN IF . . .

> It offers a variety of brewing options, including at least one pour-over method.
> The baristas look like they just stepped off the set of *Boardwalk Empire*, *Portlandia*, or *Mad Men*.
> At least eighty-five percent of the laptops being used by customers are MacBooks.
> A significant portion of the clientele is bike messengers. For reasons science cannot fully explain, bike messengers have a particularly strong nose for picking out quality coffee, and the Venn diagram between cool coffee culture and cool bike culture overlaps significantly.
> It roasts its own beans.
> It has a rotating lineup of "guest" roasters.

> The menu offers at least one single-origin coffee.
> The varieties of coffee on the menu come with short, evocative, and slightly bizarre tasting notes, like "hibiscus, citrus, Fruity Pebbles," and "green apple, dark chocolate, potpourri."
> The pastries come from high-end, local, artisan bakeries, and a slice of toast with house-made cream cheese costs $6. Sure, it's a rip-off, but if they care about where they source their food, they probably care even more about where they source their coffee.
> There are barista competition trophies on display.
> There is mysterious Japanese and European brewing equipment for sale.
> Music is played only on vinyl or cassette.
> There is a live DJ.
> It is a hybrid coffee shop and record store.
> Espresso is served with a small glass of sparkling water on the side.
> Design magazines, Mason jars, taxidermy.

KEEP WALKING IF . . .
> The baristas look like they just stepped off the set of *Jersey Shore* or *The Big Bang Theory*.
> More than one drink on the menu involves whipped cream.
> The barista re-steams a pitcher of milk. This is a big no-no, but a common one seen in crappy cafés. Like fries and kebabs, steamed milk just does not taste good reheated.
> There is a TV.
> The room smells like something's burning. This usually means they use over-roasted beans. Or the café is on fire. Either way, you don't want to go there.

- The word "expresso" is written or spoken anywhere in the store.
- Negative bonus points: the phrase "cup of chino" is written or spoken anywhere in the store.
- There are more than twenty coffee varieties available. *Some* options are good, too many options means they're probably not using freshly roasted beans.
- There are drinks with cutesy names like "Livin' La Vida Mocha" and "Whole Latte Love."
- There is a guy with an acoustic guitar playing Counting Crows covers.
- It is a hybrid coffee shop and Internet café.
- It is located inside a chain bookstore.
- There are more flavored syrup options than milk options.
- Dream catchers, prayer flags, incense.

What to Do Once You're There

If you have ever had the pleasure of being a "regular" in a bar, you know the benefits such a prestigious title can bring. Sure, there's the occasional free drink, maybe you get served a bit quicker, and you might even get your pick of the jukebox once in a while. But the real reward is being able to walk into a room full of friendly faces any night of the week, where you can shoot the shit for hours with people who are basically paid to talk to you. Your "regular" coffee shop should be no different. Once you have found a respectable establishment, make it your home base of operations for a while, and try to absorb as much knowledge and experience as possible.

In a bar, the regulars get to know the bartenders by coming in during the quiet hours, early in the week. You can show up at a bar every Friday night at 9 P.M. for a year and the bartenders still won't know you from the next drunk idiot taking too long to order their rum and Coke. The people who get treated like part of the furniture? They come in at 5 P.M. on a Tuesday. Adopt the same strategy with your chosen coffee shop. Find the off-peak times when the café is slow, and the staff is available to chat a little—that may be 11:30 A.M. on a weekday, or 3 P.M. on a weekend—and try to go at that time.

Of course, it will also help if the staff and other coffee bar flies actually like you. You don't have to name your firstborn after the store's espresso blend, just don't act like a jerk. Ways to not act like a jerk include tipping $1 on every drink (yes, every drink; forget your twenty percent, it's $1; don't make excuses, it's $1, suck it up); bussing your own cups; not interrupting the baristas when they are with other customers; not asking to change the music; not ordering labor-intensive drinks during rush hour; saying "please" and "thank you." Basically, act like your mother—if your mother tipped $1 on drinks (she doesn't, but she's old and prefers Coconut Crème Coffee-mate, anyway, bless her heart).

Taste as widely as possible. Try every drink on the menu. Try new beans whenever they bring in different varieties. Try the same beans with different preparation methods. Ask questions when you can: What would *you* use to brew this particular coffee? Is Nicaraguan coffee usually this acidic? Do you mind showing me how you pour the water into that Chemex? How many days ago was this roasted? Once we move on to the home-brewing section of coffee geekery, having cultivated this go-to source of information and advice will really start to pay off. Also, y'know, you might even meet some cool people.

And if you get on their nerves, well, they're hardly going to tell you about it if they want to keep raking in those big $1 tips.

The Myth of the Snooty Barista

One enduring stereotype about third-wave coffee shops is that they're all staffed by frowny-faced arrogant baristas who hate you and your drink preferences. It is the joke behind the (admittedly very funny) "Hipster Barista" meme that showed up a few years back, featuring a bearded and tatted barista wearing a scarf over a V-neck T-shirt with captions like "$120,000 art degree / Draws faces in latte foam" and "Puts coffee deal on Groupon / Rolls eyes when you actually use it."

Are *some* baristas like this? Sure. Some grocery stores, plant nurseries, auto repair shops, movie theaters, and banks also employ assholes. But *in my experience*, people who work in coffee shops are generally pretty nice. In my experience, people who say they constantly encounter snooty baristas are either suffering from confirmation bias (see also: people who say they are constantly being lectured to by sanctimonious vegans; people who say their SUV is constantly in danger of being run off the road by crazed cyclists), or they are going in with the expectation of snooty service, and are actually the ones acting like jerks to begin with.

Try not to approach the experience expecting to be judged or ignored. Expect that the barista wants to make you a delicious drink that you will enjoy—and that you can help them do just that by being polite and clear about what you are looking for. If you're worried about them judging you on appearance, try to extend them the same courtesy—giant ear piercings or bow ties are silly, yes, but not in and of themselves signs that you are about to receive bad service. If after all that they are still a jerk, well yeah, go elsewhere and leave a scathing Yelp review.

Drink Styles You Need to Know—and Ones You Don't

The second-wave of coffee brought with it bloated menus full of dessert-style drinks that require a spoon and half a day's worth of calories to get through. Mercifully, today's high-end coffee shops tend toward minimalist menus that focus on a handful of standard espresso drinks and a few brewed options. You should sample your way through most of them—but not all of them. In fact, some could do irreparable damage to your coffee credibility. Let's break down the drinks you will commonly see on menus.

Espresso (the Method)

Baristas may earn minimum wage, but let there be no doubt about it—making good espresso is a real skill. Not only does it require top of the line equipment kept in impeccable condition (along with great, freshly roasted, freshly ground coffee beans), but every stage of the process—from the grind size to the extraction time—needs to be seriously precise.

An espresso machine works by forcing highly pressurized hot water through a tight "puck" of coffee grounds. The result is a drink that is far more concentrated, rich, aromatic, and intense than its brewed brethren. The coffee's best qualities are enhanced—but so are its worst.

If you have only ever consumed espresso in concert with half a liter of milk and enough sugar to induce a diabetic coma in an eastern lowland gorilla, you may not realize just how bad it can be when any one of these elements is off. There is nowhere to hide.

So good espresso is worth paying good money for. And if you're paying for the best, it's worth consuming it in a form that will let you actually enjoy everything it has to offer. You wouldn't slather a premium quality steak in barbecue sauce. You wouldn't put Pètrus in a wine spritzer. Don't order great espresso like a moron.

Espresso Drinks You Need to Know

ESPRESSO (THE DRINK)

It is a testament to the all-around bad-assery of the straight espresso shot that it is served in a cup that looks like it was plucked from a five-year-old's tea set, and yet it is by far the most legit of all espresso drinks. Like a straight shot of whiskey, it's short, intense, and not for the weak of heart. But it is also the best way to truly taste all the flavors in an espresso drink, and you're going to need to down some eventually to become a true coffee proficient. You can start with the following milkier variations and work your way up to this, or you can just grow a pair and keep throwing back espressos until you can handle the pain and finally appreciate all the myriad flavors contained in that tiny two- or three-ounce cup. If nothing else, drinking it will make others respect you and keep you buzzed for hours.

MACCHIATO

No matter what certain global caffeinated-beverage empires say, a real macchiato is basically a shot of espresso with a little bit of steamed milk in it—the name in Italian literally means "marked" by milk. It still packs a strong espresso punch. So if you're too soft to handle straight espresso, the milk really takes the harsh edge off the drink, while still allowing you to experience most of the flavors and aromas of the coffee. Best of all, it comes in the same little cup as an espresso—called a "demitasse," by the way—so you can still *pretend* to be drinking espresso, at least.

FOAMING AT THE MOUTH

Terms you will hear quite often in the coffee world are "wet foam" and "dry foam." Wait, isn't all milk foam "wet?" Yes, smartass. But in espresso speak, the terms "wet" and "dry" foam—or "microfoam" and "macrofoam," respectively—refer to the texture of the steamed milk that tops off most espresso drinks. Dry foam refers to the stiff froth you might have seen floating on top of cappuccinos and macchiatos—the kind that gives you a fluffy mustache when you drink it. Wet foam refers to the velvety, textured milk that pours straight into the coffee and is most readily identified with lattes.

Well, in the past, anyway. These days, most good cafés use microfoam for just about every drink.

Though they're definitely out of vogue, some people prefer dry macchiatos and caps because they allow you to enjoy the espresso and milk separately, or mix them together to your preference. If that's your thing, you can specify a "dry cappuccino" when you order—though be prepared to be met with a withering look from the barista.

CORTADO

Though not *all* that different from a macchiato, this drink is supposed to be more akin to a tiny latte—usually about four ounces, and served in a dainty little glass. This one gets bonus points for its exoticness—originally hailing from Spain, it is a bit less common to see it on menus in the United States. You might also hear this called a "piccolo latte," which is an Australian term that has spread along with Aussie baristas who have escaped from their prison island.

GIBRALTAR

The story of this drink goes something like this: The owner of Blue Bottle Coffee in San Francisco bought a bunch of four-and-a-half-ounce glass tumblers known as Gibraltar glasses, which he used for testing and sampling behind the bar. Regulars caught wind of the tiny latte drinks, and it became something of a secret menu item. Word spread, and now you see the term "Gibraltar" popping up in cafés all over the English-speaking world. For all intents and purposes, though, it is just a cortado by another name. It is a drink you need to know because it is a fairly standard piece of café lore at this point, but don't order one if it's not on the menu unless you want to look like a total poseur.

CAPPUCCINO

When it comes to the milkier espresso drinks, most people are either latte drinkers or cappuccino drinkers, so you will need to pick a side and be prepared to defend it *to the death*.

The cappuccino is the more sophisticated choice. One part espresso, one part steamed milk, and one part foam served in a 5- to 6-ounce ceramic cup, it is the milky espresso drink of balance and moderation. It is also the milky espresso drink of heritage and history, with a name that supposedly dates back to the seventeenth century. If you order a cappuccino in Italy today, the drink you receive won't be so very different from what you would get in a good U.S. coffee shop.

LATTE

If the cappuccino is the sophisticated, European choice, the latte is the f*** you, I'm American and I'll drink my coffee as I goddamn please choice.

Coffee know-it-alls love to lecture latte orderers that asking for a "latte" in Italy will just get you a cup of milk ("latte" means "milk" in Italian, so that makes pretty good sense), and that the "correctly" named drink, "caffe latte," is consumed only with breakfast—certainly never as an afternoon pick-me-up, and certainly never in the obscenely large cups we use here. Well, Italians also don't have garlic bread or put pepperoni on their pizzas, so who's really missing out there? It is your deity-given right as an American to consume any foodstuffs you feel like at any time of the day or night in whatever sized cup you want.

In *this* country, a latte is typically served in a 12-ounce ceramic cup (except in strip mall coffee chains, where it is served in a bucket) with a shot (or two) of espresso, topped with steamed milk, and finished off with a little bit of foam.

LATTE ARTISTS

● ● ●

With well-textured microfoam, a skilled barista can draw designs and patterns in the top of an espresso drink while they pour (sometimes with the extra help of a tea-spoon). This is known as "latte art," though it can be done in cappuccinos and even macchiatos. For a while there, really elaborate latte art seemed to go out of vogue with minimalist-loving third-wavers, in favor of simple rosetta and heart motifs. But an increasing number of cafés and baristas seem to be loosening up and embracing funny and creative designs again, and we're starting to see more birds, lions, and flowers back in the mix. As of 2014, the United States Coffee Championships—the biggest and most prestigious competitive coffee event in the country—added a U.S. Latte Art Championship to its roster, which means cutesy animals in your coffee are definitely becoming socially acceptable once again. Rejoice!

AMERICANO

While we're talking Americans bastardizing espresso drinks, let's talk about the Americano—that's a shot of espresso topped with an indefinite amount of hot water (basically, as much as it takes to fill the cup). The drink is of indeterminate origin, but was supposedly served to U.S. servicemen stationed in Europe in World War II in an effort to replicate the taste of freedom, a.k.a. drip-filter coffee.

Despite its crude beginnings, this is another option for sampling espresso—as with straight whiskey, adding a *little bit* of water can help open up the flavors and aromas of the coffee. But adding a *lot* of water, as many coffee shops do, will just dilute the whole thing and make it gross. So if you're going to go this route, ask specifically for only about five ounces of water.

FLAT WHITE

This mysterious milky espresso drink originally hails from Australia and New Zealand (like the with Pavlova cake and Russell Crowe, both countries fight bitterly over ownership), but has recently spread like wildfire throughout the United States and UK, once again thanks to those escaped-convicts-turned-baristas. Even Down Under, there isn't total consensus about what the drink actually *is*—most cafés have their own variations—but to understand it, you need to know that over there, lattes traditionally come in glass tumblers, and cappuccinos in ceramic cups topped with cocoa powder. In that context, the flat white serves as a genuine halfway point between the two—it comes in a ceramic cup, but without the cocoa topping of the cappuccino. Its purpose in the United States—beyond novelty value—is less clear. But as a rule of thumb, think of it as a latte served in a cappuccino cup. It's worth knowing because the style is having a moment, but there is no very great reason for you to go out of your way to find one.

AFFOGATO

This is espresso served over a scoop of ice cream or gelato. Okay, you don't *really* need to know this one for any serious coffee credibility reasons, but holy hell is it delicious.

Espresso Drinks You *Don't* Need to Know

MOCHA

The café mocha or mochaccino is a latte or cappuccino with cocoa mix or chocolate syrup in it—basically, caffeinated hot chocolate. No one over the age of sixteen has any business being anywhere near this drink.

VANILLA/CARAMEL/[INSERT FLAVOR HERE] LATTE

Similarly, these espresso drinks spiked with flavored syrups (and often topped with whipped cream) are for baby palates who do not actually like the taste of coffee. They are the appletinis of the coffee world. You wouldn't order a lemon drop from a craft cocktail bar; don't order a pumpkin spice latte from a craft coffee shop.

ESPRESSO CON PANNA

Also known as a café Vienna, this is espresso topped with whipped cream. Just . . . no. Whipped cream is for pie, slapstick comedy, and sex.

BABYCCINO

Though it is made using an espresso machine, this isn't even technically an espresso drink—it's a cup of steamed milk and foam, sometimes dusted with cocoa, that moms in yoga pants give small children with names like Juniper and Atticus to keep them occupied in coffee shops. On the upside, cafés that have this drink on their menu are tacitly letting you know that their establishments are frequented by such people, indicating that perhaps you should take your business elsewhere. So it does have its uses. See also: doggyccinos.

CHAI LATTE

This is not actually an espresso drink, either. It is an aromatic Indian spice and tea drink mixed with steamed milk. It can be very nice, but you are far too busy learning about coffee to waste your time drinking tea.

RED EYE

Also known as a depth charge, sledgehammer, eye opener, shot in the dark, and about eleventy-bajillion other names, this is a shot (or several shots) of espresso *in* a cup of brewed coffee. At this point, you should have learned enough to realize that this is not a recipe for good coffee, but simply a brutal caffeine delivery method. Which is fine—we've all had moments in our lives where we've considered mainlining Red Bull to stay awake—but that puts it firmly in the purview of truck drivers and college students, *not* serious coffee scholars.

Other Coffee Drinks You Need to Know

Until very recently, you were probably only visiting a coffee shop to order one of two things—an espresso drink or batch-brewed coffee self-served from a press pot. But in recent years, a small laboratory of other brewing devices have found their way onto menus. And this is a good thing. If you're trying to learn about the unique flavors and possibilities of different coffees, it makes sense to test them out in a range of preparation methods. But it does mean there are a whole lot more drinks to memorize, so let's look at which are actually worth your time and money.

POUR-OVER

If you've ever seen a barista carefully poised over a cone-shaped device with a weird-looking kettle, like an uptight gardener watering an extremely delicate flower, you have probably seen someone preparing a pour-over.

There are a number of devices that use this brewing method—from plastic or porcelain Melitta cones to slick glass Chemex flasks (and we will break these down in more detail in Chapter 5)—but the principle is the same for all of them: Grounds are placed in a conical filter (usually paper, occasionally metal); hot water is slowly added in; the resulting liquid drips through the filter, and down into a cup or container below. Smooth and light bodied, when prepared by someone who knows what they're doing, pour-overs are a fantastic way to bring out the subtle nuances and unique characteristics of different coffees.

This method of brewing is nothing new, but its popularity sure is—they've really only become a coffee shop fixture in the 2000s. So there is still a lot of inconsistency in how different establishments approach these and other manual brew methods. In some, pour-over is the default method for brewed coffee and is priced accordingly. The coffee shop will probably have a "bar" of brewers set up to handle multiple drinks simultaneously, and possibly even a barista dedicated to handling these drinks alone.

In other coffee shops, it is considered more of a special offering that you have to request, in which case it is also usually priced accordingly—high. This isn't unreasonable; pour-over coffee is labor-intensive and each drink eats up several minutes of a barista's time. But if it looks like they're just keeping a dusty old brewer on a shelf in case someone asks for one, you might want to pass; you don't want to pay $7 for a half-assed job.

If you plan on playing with pour-over brewers at home, it's definitely worth tracking down a place that does it really well. Being able to observe the right preparation and pouring method—and having the chance to try a number of different styles of pour-over in one place—is invaluable (and by "invaluable," I mean you won't waste time and money trying to copy it ineptly from YouTube videos back in your kitchen).

SIPHON

The siphon or vacuum coffeemaker (or sometimes vac pot) was invented in Germany way back in the 1830s (or France in the 1840s, depending on whom you ask), and actually enjoyed some popularity in the United States in the early 1900s, yet all but disappeared from these shores in the latter half of the twentieth century. It came roaring back into vogue in the late 2000s, when some third-wave coffee shops started mimicking the eye-catching siphon bars found in Japanese coffee shops. These setups can cost a hefty chunk of change, and the method is quite labor intensive, so the siphon's cachet seems to have waned a bit as cafés have moved toward cheaper manual brew methods. But if you see it on offer, you should definitely try it out because siphon coffee tastes great and it looks even cooler.

The basic idea is this: There are two glass containers, with a gasket and a filter in between them. Water goes in the bottom one, and coffee in the top. Some sort of heat source (la-di-da machines might have a halogen burner, cheap ones a little alcohol lamp) is placed below the bottom container, heating the water. The water vapors push the liquid up into the top chamber, brewing the coffee. When the heat is turned off, the bottom container cools, creating a vacuum and pulling the liquid back down through the filter.

The resulting cup is super clean, but with all the flavors of the coffee pronounced and enhanced. And did I mention how cool it looks? It looks really cool.

COLD BREW

Along with jorts and headwear appropriated from Native Americans, ice-filled plastic cups of cold brew coffee have become the de rigueur summertime accessories of the early 2010s—go to any trendy neighborhood in the country around mid-July, and you'll see Coachella chicks and Bonnaroo boys sucking it up by the straw-full as they stroll between brunch spots and Urban Outfitters. But unlike faux-vintage designer cut-off jeans and sorority girls with feathers in their hair, cold brew is a fashion trend that is actually worth celebrating.

Ironically, the most common method for making cold brew is just about as uncool as it gets—it is usually done in a big plastic bucket. The coffee steeps in there for anywhere between twelve and twenty-four hours, then drips out through a filter in the bottom into a highly concentrated brew. Cafés typically keep the concentrate in a pitcher in the fridge, then just cut it with cold water in a cup to order. Though some are now getting fancy and putting it in kegs, then serving it up on tap like a beer.

Cold brew's exploding popularity is great because it is surreptitiously introducing many newcomers to the delights of manually brewed and single-origin coffees. Cold brew is so mild and smooth, it is easy to drink without sugar and milk. And though the flavors tend to be fairly simple, they're also straightforward and easy to identify. Think of it as a gateway drug. A delicious, refreshing gateway drug.

KYOTO

When I said cold brew is *usually* made in a plastic bucket, this is the exception, and it deserves its own subhead because it is so damn cool (pun intended). Kyoto-style cold brew is made in tall towers—totem poles of glass pipes and chambers that can

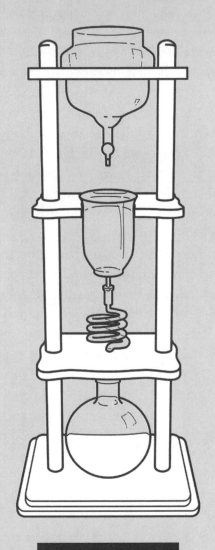

A Kyoto drip tower.

reach up to three-and-a-half feet, and look like something out of a movie-set science lab. Water goes in the top chamber, then slowly and gently drips down onto coffee grounds and through a filter, then drips through *more* tubes and eventually into a container below. It looks and sounds painfully tedious, and can take anywhere from eight to twenty-four hours, depending on the height of the brewer and the drip rate. The final product is typically a bit more complex and sweeter than fully steeped cold brew, though not always dramatically different. Mostly, it just looks more awesome.

HOT-BREWED COLD BREW

The name may sound like a contradiction, but one of the newest trends in summertime coffee making is to brew hot coffee directly over ice. Also called "Japanese iced coffee," this is usually done as a pour-over—either with a drip cone or a Chemex. Some cafés are now experimenting with an AeroPress as well. This method allows the hot water just enough contact time to bring the aromatics and acidity out in the coffee, before it passes through the filter and hits the ice. The ice cools and dilutes the brew, but the characteristics of the hot-brewed coffee remain.

This is great for people who find cold brew too mellow or one-note, as well as those who just can't bring themselves to pay a barista $3 to pour their drink out of a pitcher.

AUTOMATED SINGLE-CUP BREWERS

In its short history, the third-wave coffee industry seems to have struggled between embracing technological innovation in the pursuit of ever more perfect coffee, and maintaining its handmade, artisanal ethos. Little embodies this tension better than the story of the Clover. The machine was released in 2007 by a group of Stanford engineers, who combined the technology of a French press and a siphon into one (mostly) automated system.

Each machine cost $11,000.

For about five minutes (okay, a year), it was the toast of the coffee industry. Chicago's Intelligentsia bought several, as did Portland's Stumptown, Café Grumpy in New York, and Caffe Vita in Seattle. Then, in 2008, the company was bought out by Starbucks, and the indies couldn't get rid of their Clovers fast enough. About a year later, everyone seemed to be switching to cheap plastic pour-overs and using the phrase "handcrafted" a lot.

You'll rarely find a Clover outside of a Starbucks these days (which is actually a shame, because they can make a really nice cup), but recently, newer machines that brew single cups of coffee seem to be making a comeback in the third-wave world. Ultimately, coffee geeks are, well, geeks, and technology is capable of a level of precision that humans aren't, so we will probably all have to bow down to our coffee-making robot overlords eventually.

One such machine rapidly showing up all over the country is the Steampunk (don't be put off by the name; it has nothing to do with cosplaying neck beards), an eye-catching steel and glass contraption made by a Utah company called Alpha Dominche. It's basically a computerized siphon brewer. It allows for a level of control and consistency manual siphons don't, and is capable of making a really nice cup (in fact, several really nice cups at once, which is no doubt part of the appeal for coffee shops). It also looks damn cool.

There are a bunch of other startup tech-infused brewers out there—the BKON Craft Brewer, Blossom One Brewer, the Modbar, to name a few. Are they any good? Hell if I know—they're new. But definitely try them if you see them just so you can say you did.

Other Coffee Drinks You *Don't* Need to Know

VIETNAMESE ICED COFFEE

Ca phe sua da—or Vietnamese iced coffee with milk—makes for a great accompaniment to a bánh mì or a bowl of pho. It rarely, however, makes for a great coffee. The drink is traditionally prepared using darkly roasted beans—often Café Du Monde chicory coffee in the United States, though also frequently imported Vietnamese brands—coarsely ground, and brewed in a fairly basic little metal drip filter called a phin. These days, many eateries also just half-ass it with regular brewed or instant coffee. Either way, the coffee is then poured over ice and topped with sweetened condensed milk.

Let's be honest—ca phe sua da gets cut a lot of slack because of its interesting and exotic history as a culinary byproduct of French Indochina; if this drink were invented by Americans and served at Western coffee chains, foodies would be poo-pooing it on Chowhound. I'm not saying it doesn't taste good, I'm just saying: this drink is fifty percent sugary milk goop from a can.

FRENCH PRESS

These big plunger pots make a great cup, but this is literally one of the easiest brewing methods on Earth short of instant coffee and there is no reason you should go out of your way to pay someone to do it for you. (Okay, there is one, and that is if you are at a restaurant. Waiters and chefs are not trained baristas, thus restaurant espresso is almost invariably vile. If you want to drink coffee at the end of your meal, French press is the only method that both results in a nice drink and is almost impossible to screw up).

CAFÉ AU LAIT

"Café au lait" is fun to say because it rhymes, but it is less fun to drink. It is basically a latte with brewed coffee instead of espresso. There is one place it is acceptable to order this drink, and that is as a tourist in New Orleans, where it is the standard serving method of chicory coffee, which is the standard accompaniment to beignets. And beignets are delicious.

BOTTLED COLD BREW

Several really good roasters (and now a few not-so-great ones) make ready-to-drink bottles of cold brew coffee. It is a fine option for a picnic (assuming you can't be bothered to make your own) or if your only coffee option is a grocery store (you can generally find them in Whole Foods Markets and the like), but why go to coffee shop then pay a barista $4 to unscrew a bottle cap for you? The product is generally not quite as nice as cold brew made in small batches in-store, you're paying a premium for the bottling, and it's not environmentally friendly for cafés to open a new bottle for every single drink. Screw that.

Coffee Cuppings

If you want to learn about wine, you attend wine tastings. If you want to learn about beer, you attend beer tastings. And if you want to learn about coffee, you attend coffee ... cuppings. Hey, I didn't name it.

The practice of cupping actually dates back at least a century. Traditionally, it was (and still is) a technique performed by roasters and traders as a way to assess the quality and characteristics of the beans they were buying. With such a long history, the process has become almost comically ritualized over the years, and many purpose-built accoutrements have appeared—a standard professional cupping setup might include a specially made rotating circular table, spittoons, special spoons, cups, trays, and often even lab chairs (which add precisely nothing to the process, but look cool and certainly make you feel very serious and important while loudly slurping and spitting coffee).

Coffee education has long been a mission objective of many third-wave roasters and cafés, and at some point, some of them came up with the bright idea to make cuppings open to the public, to help the unwashed masses understand the nuances of quality coffee (and, if we're being cynical, to convince those same people of why they should pay for that quality coffee). Some coffee shops now hold regular monthly, weekly, and sometimes even daily public cuppings; others hold them more sporadically as special events. Many are free, though even the ones that cost money are typically well worth the investment at least once.

If none of the stores in your city holds cuppings, it is definitely something to consider doing next time you are in a big city with a lot of good roasters, like New York, San Francisco, Chicago, or Seattle. Bring your friends and family—they will have way more fun than they expect to, and you just might convert them away from their caramel mochas.

Public cuppings tend to be far more laid-back than their professional counterparts—don't expect lab chairs—but they still follow roughly the same rituals. Here is an idea of what to expect.

STEP ONE: PREPARING THE BEANS

The venue holding the cupping will probably pick about three or four different beans to sample. It's likely they will choose ones with distinctly different origins and taste profiles, and there are two pretty good reasons for this: firstly, these tastings—especially the ones at big-name coffee shops—tend to attract a lot of wide-eyed tourists, and showing coffee n00bs just how different a Colombian coffee is from a Rwandan one is going to be a far more mind-blowing experience than showing them two slightly different coffees from neighboring farms; but more pragmatically, most coffee shops and roasters only have four to six different beans in stock at any given time, and it would be pretty stupid for those beans to all taste the same. So they work with what they've got.

The barista running the cupping may tell you what the beans are going in, but they may also choose to do the tasting blind. Obviously, the latter method is intended to keep you from tasting the coffees with any preconceived bias, but given most people at a public cupping know squat about coffee, this isn't such an important factor.

STEP TWO: GRINDING

The barista will start boiling water, and grind equal amounts of each coffee. You will all sniff the coffee grounds. Try not to get any up your nose. You're probably not going to notice anything very significant at this stage, but feel free to make "pleasantly surprised," "intrigued," and "looking thoughtfully into the distance" faces as you smell to make yourself look more knowledgeable and psych-out your fellow tasters.

STEP THREE: BREWING

Once the water is ready, the barista will slowly pour it onto the grounds in each cup. Some cupping sessions will have you sniff again at this point, but more likely, you're just going to wait three to five minutes while the coffee brews in the cup and everyone makes awkward small talk.

STEP FOUR: BREAKING THE CRUST

By the time the coffee has brewed, the grounds will have formed a thick crust on top of the cup, and you will have heard more than you care to know about your fellow taster Irene's daughter's nail salon in Council Bluffs, Iowa. Now the real fun begins—and not just because Irene is finally going to have to shut up. You're going to get right down close to the cup, with your nose right over it, and stick a spoon into the crust, breaking through to the liquid below. Push the crust back while inhaling the aromas that waft up out of the cup. Move quickly around to the next cup—someone else will have already broken that crust, but there should still be a lot of things to sniff. Repeat across every cup. Yes, you will all look pretty stupid bent over sticking your noses into cups. Yes, you will probably get coffee crust on your nose.

STEP FIVE: TASTING

Once you're done smelling, either you or the barista will remove the remaining crust from the cups. It is almost time to taste, but first: wash your dirty spoon, you filthy animal. The barista will provide a cup of water to facilitate this, and you should wash your spoon in it between every cup. Not only will it prevent cross contamination between coffees, but it will prevent cross contamination between you and Irene.

The "correct" method of tasting the coffee is to take a spoonful from the cup, and slurp it as loudly and aggressively as possible. No, seriously. Sucking the coffee into your mouth like that sprays it evenly across your tongue and sends it up into your nasal cavities, letting you taste and smell it at the same time. You may have seen wine tasters do this too, but coffee tasters do it way more loudly and obnoxiously for some reason.

Real cuppers also always spit out their drink. You probably won't have to, but you will be given the choice. Spitting will make it easier to clear your palate after each sip, but there is unlikely to be an actual spittoon at a public cupping, so it probably also means you have to spit into a cup, then carry that backwash spit cup around with you for the rest of the session. Between the coffee crust on your nose and the vigorous slurping sounds around you, however, your benchmark for humiliation may have changed.

STEP SIX: MORE TASTING, AND TALKING

You are going to sample every coffee several times. As the coffee cools, the flavors will change, and you must continue to slurp, slurp, slurp until you've tasted the rainbow of coffee flavors.

Traditionally, people do not talk or compare tasting notes until the end of the cupping. If Irene says she can taste Wildberry Toaster Strudel, you might suddenly find yourself saying, "Oh, yeah, wild berry . . ." even though you had previously been getting more of a Brown Sugar Cinnamon Pop-Tarts vibe. But public cuppings sometimes disregard this rule in favor of encouraging people to identify flavors as soon as they taste them. Either way, at some point, it will come time to share your thoughts with the class. Your barista will tell you that there are no "wrong" descriptors. But what they really mean by that is that they will respond to tasting notes they agree with by saying, "Yep, definitely some of that in there," and ones they don't with, "Hmmm . . . okay, sure."

Identifying individual characteristics in coffee is tricky at first. But don't be that dickhead who says, "Uh, it tastes like coffee?" Concentrate on the flavors and aromas, and the way the drink feels in your mouth. You don't need to identify everything, just try to hone in on a single characteristic like listening to a song and just trying to pinpoint the bassline.

There is nothing wrong with saying, "It reminds me of the brownies at my middle school cafeteria," but given it's unlikely anyone else in the cupping went to your middle school, that kind of observation may not be terribly instructive. So here is a cheat sheet to help you turn the weird things you can taste, smell, and feel into coffee speak:

REMINDS ME OF: SAY THIS

> Smells like a Jamba Juice store: Tropical fruit.
> Tastes like a Snickers bar: Nutty and chocolaty.
> Makes my mouth slick like I've just eaten a $1 slice of pizza: Buttery.
> Smells like that air freshener Mom sprays in the bathroom: Floral.
> Tastes like my mouth on a Sunday morning: Tobacco, ashy.

> Tastes like my mouth on a Saturday morning: Winey.
> Smells like that bachelor/bachelorette party I still can't quite remember: Leathery.
> Feels like I have dry mouth: Astringent.
> Tastes like my tongue after licking a nine-volt battery to see if it's still working: Alkaline.
> Smells like, err, a certain herbal refreshment: Leguminous, alliaceous.
> Tastes like IHOP: Syrup-like, caramel-y.
> Tastes like Christmas cookies: Brown sugar sweetness.
> Smells like paint thinner: Turpentine-y.

Further Reading

> "Left Coast Roast" (*www.leftcoastroast.com*) is an excellent guide to great coffee roasters and shops in Northern California, Oregon, and Washington, and the folks behind them. If you live in that area or are headed that way, it will guide you to some wonderful coffee-drinking experiences, and some equally wonderful people.

> *Eater* (*www.eater.com*) is a large network of city-based food news blogs, and basically the restaurant industry's version of *The Hollywood Reporter*. Many of the city blogs offer a recurring feature called "Where to Drink Coffee in [City] Right Now," which is usually a decent—if not definitive—guide to the better coffee outfits in any given city.

> "33 Cups of Coffee" (*www.33books.com*) is more accurately described as further writing than reading. These little pocket notebooks allow you to keep a record of different coffees you

try, with space for tasting notes, details such as the roast date and brew method, and even a flavor wheel on each page. Gimmicky? Sure, but they only cost $4 each, and the novelty might even help you coax friends and family into joining in with one of your home cuppings.

> *Counter Culture Coffee* (*www.counterculturecoffee.com*) has made an incredibly thorough and eye-catching "Coffee Taster's Flavor Wheel" that you can download and print out for free from its website. It is full of really evocative and hyper-specific descriptors to impress your friends with, like "lemon grass," "sweet bread pastry," and "soy sauce."

FIVE

Start Brewing at Home

Now you know what good coffee tastes like. You've seen it being made. It's time to start making some yourself.

Some coffee nerds make all their coffee at home, and only go into coffee shops to buy beans; others continue to purchase many of their drinks from cafés. As your mother told you before you became aware of the crushing reality of the job market, college fees, and your own intellectual and physical limitations: you can be anything you want to be. *But* at this point in time, it is probably a good idea to withdraw a bit from the coffee shop scene to work on your own barista skills. Not only do you need to practice if you actually want to get any good, but cutting back on those $4 cortados will help you save some money to buy your own coffee-making gear.

Things You Will Need (and a Few Things You Won't)

Access to good coffee should be a basic human right. But sadly, until the government or United Nations recognizes this, you're going to have to shell out some of your own hard earned to get your daily (hourly?) fix.

Making good coffee at home is ultimately cheaper than buying it in cafés, but you will still have to invest some capital up front. There are some items you can avoid buying—for now—and some you can't. Here is a breakdown of the gear you definitely need right this second, and the gear you can probably relegate to your Amazon Wish List.

A Coffeemaker

Well, duh. We'll get to the specifics shortly.

A Grinder

Of all the equipment investments you make in your pursuit of true coffee nerdery, this is the most important. That may sound illogical: surely the coffeemaker itself is the most essential thing? Nope. You can get away with a $20 coffee brewer. You cannot get away with a $20 grinder.

And let's get this out of the way first: you *must* buy a grinder.

The more surface area coffee beans have, the quicker they lose flavor and aroma. Grinding them up into really tiny pieces? That's a lot of surface area. Just like a good coffee shop, you want to grind your beans to order so you can enjoy them at their best. So no buying pre-ground coffee, no grinding your coffee at the grocery store. You have to grind at home.

There are two types of grinders: blade grinders and burr grinders. Let's get to know them.

BLADE GRINDERS

All you need to know about blade grinders is that they are rubbish and you shouldn't buy one.

Okay, a little more detail on that: Blade grinders are the ones with two little right-angled blades that whir around like a vicious propeller. If you have a coffee grinder in your house already, it is almost certainly a blade grinder. Throw it out. (Or keep it as a spice mill. Whatever).

Blade grinders are cheap and barbaric. They hack the beans up crudely and indiscriminately, turning some to dust and leaving others partially intact. This is a problem, because coffee needs to be ground uniformly—both so the flavor is extracted evenly from each particle, and so you don't end up with dirty grounds in your cup. To make matters worse, blade grinders can also generate a lot of heat and friction, leaving the coffee tasting burnt.

In other words: They are literally the worst.

BURR GRINDERS

You probably own several burr grinders already, albeit manual ones: your salt and pepper mills. Yep, you've been using a more superior grinder for your seasonings than for your coffee.

Burr grinders basically pulverize beans into equal sizes by crushing them between two metal surfaces. Conical burr grinders do this via a cone-shaped mechanism with spiky ridges on it, while flat burr grinders do this between two round plates with spiky ridges on them. Both work great, though you tend to find conical burrs only on more expensive machines. And burr grinders do get really expensive—starting at about $100 for something passable, and going up into the thousands for commercial-grade equipment.

A conical burr grinder.

The high-end machines have all sorts of bells and whistles (and, of course, tend to be made of higher quality and more durable materials), but the most significant difference between the cheaper and more expensive models may be the motor—budget machines typically have high-speed motors, and fancy machines low-speed motors. The latter is optimal because fast motors generate more heat, but don't stress about this too much at first; you can still start making some really nice coffee with a more economical burr grinder, then upgrade when you find the cash.

Other decisions you will have to make in purchasing a burr grinder are:

STEPPED VS. STEPLESS

Different brewers use different grind sizes. These aren't serving suggestions, they're more like video game formats—you can put an Xbox disc in a PC, but it won't let you play Call of Duty. Similarly, you can put really finely ground beans in a French press, and, okay, it will still make coffee, but it's going to be pretty gross coffee. (This is another reason you don't want to buy pre-ground coffee in stores—you're stuck with a whole bag of coffee that will only work in certain types of brewer.) So you don't *just* want to buy a good grinder, you want to buy a good grinder that is specifically good at the grind sizes you need.

A stepped grinder has a bunch of preset grind sizes (anywhere from maybe nine to over fifty), and a knob or dial you turn to select the one you want. A stepless grinder, as the name suggests, has no such "steps"—you can dial it in to an infinite number of sizes.

The pros and cons of both styles should be pretty obvious: Stepped grinders are easier to use, and are less of a pain in the ass if you often switch between grind sizes, but your options are limited—wish you could make that one setting just a *little* bit finer? You can't. Stepless grinders, on the other hand, offer far more flexibility and room for experimentation, but they're more complicated and may be intimidating to beginners—how can you pinpoint the perfect AeroPress grind when you don't even know the ballpark range you're playing in?

DOSING VS. NON-DOSING

If you've ever watched a barista in a coffee shop grinding coffee for an espresso drink (and by this point, I sure hope you have, many times), you probably have seen them pull a lever sideways—hearing a distinct "click" with each pull—resulting in a small load of grounds being dumped out into the portafilter (that's the filter with the handle that goes into the espresso machine) below.

That's a dosing grinder. When you put the beans in and turn the machine on, the grounds don't automatically come out the other end. Instead, they get collected in a round chamber, separated out into seven-gram compartments (you know that little plastic wheel thingy you move around the board in Trivial Pursuit? It's like that, but you don't have to answer impossible geography questions to fill it). Each time the lever is pulled, the chamber rotates, and one compartment—or "dose"—falls through a hole and into whatever receptacle you are holding below.

A non-dosing grinder is more like a wood chipper: beans go in, and the grounds just keep coming out until you press the off switch. It's messier (though many do have some sort of container built in to catch the grounds), but more flexible.

Really, the dosing mechanism is largely useful for people making espresso (spoiler alert: that isn't going to be you) in large quantities (again, not you). In short: you don't *need* a dosing grinder at home. But at least now you know what that clicking sound is.

HAND GRINDERS

Hand-cranked grinders are awesome. They use burrs, they're relatively cheap, they're highly portable, and they let you see the basic mechanics of coffee grinding in action. The catch is that you have to power them with your own bare hands, a process that is both tedious and surprisingly exhausting.

Look, in the long run, you don't want to be using a hand grinder for the majority of your coffee making. Imagine bringing a date home "for coffee," then spending the next twenty minutes frantically turning a crank like a speed-addled hurdy-gurdy player.

But if you simply can't afford a good electric burr grinder, a hand grinder is *still* preferable to a blade grinder or buying preground coffee. And making coffee will become such a pain in the ass, it will give you more incentive to beg, borrow, or steal to get the money for something better.

A hand mill will set you back anywhere from $40 to $100. The more expensive ones tend to have wood and metal cases, while the cheaper ones are housed in plastic, but both actually work really well. They come in stepped and stepless models, and with flat and conical burrs, but obviously they are all non-dosing—you'll know when you've ground enough because your arm will get sore and you'll say, "Good enough."

Beans

Making coffee requires coffee beans. See Chapter 6 for information about where and how to buy them—and buy good ones.

Scales

You can't bake a nice loaf of bread or become a successful drug dealer without a good scale. But can you make good coffee without weighing everything first?

Let's go back to that nice loaf of bread. As most professional bakers will tell you, the biggest mistake most people make when making bread or cake at home is measuring their ingredients by volume (in a measuring cup or spoon) instead of by weight (on a food scale). Four ounces of flour on a scale is a precise measurement. But a cup of flour is an imprecise measurement—the type of flour, the way it has been stored, and whether it has been sifted or not can all affect what volume of the measuring cup it occupies. Beans are the same—different origins, varietals, processing methods, and roasting styles will all affect the density of the coffee you buy. And that's even if you could fill a teaspoon measuring scoop to the *exact* same level each time, which, sorry, you can't.

So the best way to measure out your coffee accurately every time? By weight. On the scale.

Measuring water by volume is obviously far more accurate. But! Measuring before boiling is no good because you're going to lose some water to steam, and measuring after is problematic because the water will start to cool while you mess around pouring it back and forth. A better way is to put the actual brewing device on the scale, then measure by weight as you fill it up. Then there is no time wasted, and no margin for error.

Some brewing methods (say, French press) are a little more forgiving without a scale than others (pour-over), but it's never a bad idea to be consistent and accurate. You're also going to have far less coffee waste, saving you money in the long run.

WHAT TO LOOK FOR IN SCALES

There are some fancy-pants scales out there designed specifically for coffee making, which include special features like inbuilt timers and drip trays. There is even one now with a smartphone app that gives you feedback on your pouring technique. If you have $150 to blow on a scale like that, go ahead and do it, but you don't *need* to. When starting out, you should be able to get something fine for $20. You do, however, need a scale that has the following features:

> It should be digital (in other words: no, you can't substitute your bathroom scale);

> It should display measurements in grams;

> It should be accurate to at least ½ gram;

> It should have a "tare" function—so when you put your brewer on the scale and press that button, the scale will automatically reset to zero, subtracting the weight on top;

> It should *not* turn off after a set time (probably thirty seconds) or it should at least have the ability to override that function. Many brewing methods require you to pour in water slowly over the space of several minutes, so obviously the scale needs to stay on for that entire time.

Cups

Like, literally, you will need some cups out of which to drink your coffee. Of course, there are cups out there made especially for coffee, but will they significantly impact your enjoyment? Nope. Sure, those probably retain heat a little better, maybe aid in the distribution of aromas a bit, but you definitely don't *need* them. If you already own a coffee mug, it is probably fine so long as there is nothing growing in it.

The exception here is espresso drinks, especially the shorter ones like espresso and macchiatos—trying to drink those out of regular cups is awkward and unpleasant. So if you do go down the treacherous and ill-advised home-espresso path, you will need to buy some of those. But for brewed coffee, that mug you got for free with your car insurance is totally fine.

Carafes

If you're planning on making large quantities of coffee—either for several people or because you want to make a few cups at once for yourself—you may need to decant your coffee into another container to keep it hot and/or to stop it from continuing to brew. You'll want to do this when using a larger-sized pour-over or French press.

There are special glass carafes out there—they typically retail in the $15 to $35 range—but if aesthetics and shape aren't important, you can just use a thermos or recycle the pot from an old drip coffeemaker.

Kettle

No matter what your brewing method, you are going to need a water-boiling apparatus, and a pot or microwave just isn't going to cut it. For some brewing methods, the kettle you have in your kitchen right now will be fine. Others, however, require you to pour in hot water very slowly and precisely, and that cheap old hunk of metal sitting on your stove won't do because the spout is almost certainly too large and short for you to exercise any control.

In these cases, it's a pretty good idea to invest in a specialty "gooseneck" (sometimes "swan-neck") kettle—so named because they sport a long, thin, curved spout that looks a *little* like a goose's neck (if that goose happened to be curving its neck while also balancing at a right angle, which seems like an admittedly unlikely scenario.) You can buy these online or from coffee equipment stores. The cheaper stovetop models start at about $30, while the electric ones will set you back at least $60. Some of the electric ones allow you to specify exact temperatures *and* maintain that temperature while resting for some time, which is really neat if you have the cash to splash on those sorts of perks.

Filters

It's easy to overlook the humble filter, but your purchasing decisions here can actually have a big impact on the ultimate taste and quality of the coffee you brew. Some brewers—like the French press, moka pot, and some siphon models—have inbuilt filters, so it's just one less thing you have to worry about. But most paper filters come in a variety of choices. Some brewers are compatible with a range of brands, so you will have extra decisions to make there around price and availability. Others only work with specific paper filters sold by their manufacturers. Either way, the one common decision you will be faced with is whether to buy "natural" brown filters or bleached white filters. This is basically an ethical choice. Many people find that brown filters can impart a "papery" taste in the coffee, but the white filters are a bit less environmentally friendly (in so much as throwing away paper every time you make coffee is at all environmentally friendly). At the very least, look for white filters that are oxygen bleached, rather than chlorine bleached—which most of the major brands these days are, anyway.

A third option with many brewers now is to buy a reusable metal filter. This will lessen the environmental impact of your coffee, but be aware that these filters can dramatically affect the drink's taste. This isn't necessarily a bad thing—the stainless steel filters made for the Chemex, for instance, have developed a strong fan base precisely *because* they result in a fuller-bodied, more flavorful cup than the standard paper filters made by the company— just be aware that you're signing up for something different.

Thermometer

Water boils at 212°F, but the optimal water temperature for brewing is between 195°F and 205°F. You can just wait a minute after boiling for the water to cool slightly and hope it's the right temperature, or you can buy a thermometer and be sure. You'll want something waterproof and fast acting, which you should be able to find for about $15.

Water

Most coffee drinks are at least ninety-eight percent water. If you make coffee with gross water, the final drink is still going to taste gross. If the tap water in your city is gross (*cough*, Las Vegas, *cough*), then you need to filter your water first.

Choose Your Brew

Ultimately, you should aim to master several brewing styles (or at least have a working knowledge sufficient to wax bullshit about them for a few minutes). But the easiest way to up your coffee skills in the shortest amount of time is to choose one method and completely steep yourself (pun intended) in it. Honestly, if you're really lazy, you can just pick one method to nail and be done with it—just as long as you learn enough about how it works and why you like it so you can defend your preference when arguing with other caffeine geeks, of course. But you still want to make an informed choice about which method that will be.

Obviously taste and quality should be a big factor in your decision-making process, but you can learn to love anything if you drink it enough. Price, convenience, difficulty, and how cool it makes you by association should all be considerations, too. You don't choose shoes or cars for comfort alone (or possibly at all), so don't think of this purchase any differently.

But before we look at your options, let's have a heart-to-heart about espresso machines.

ESPRESSO MACHINES AND WHY
YOU SHOULDN'T BUY ONE

Let's get this out of the way first: You think you want a home espresso machine. But you do not want a home espresso machine.

Most of the other coffee-making devices you will use are pretty lo-fi: they don't have many moving parts, don't use particularly sophisticated technologies, and even the cheapest model is probably pretty serviceable. Espresso machines are, well, machines. The quality of the drink they produce is directly proportional to the quality of the machine. Martin Scorsese can't record a great feature film on a flip phone camera, and even a champion barista can't make a great espresso on a $250 machine from Walmart.

So that's reason number one: price. Good quality home espresso machines *start* at about $700, and only go up from there. You will also need a pricey electric burr grinder to get a fine enough grind, so that's even more money.

Reason number two? Degree of difficulty. There's a reason your favorite third-wave coffee shop hires only professional baristas with experience at other third-wave coffee shops, while giant chains hire bored sixteen-year-olds: making espresso drinks *well* is a skill. Even once you're working with professional gear, it takes a lot of training and practice. In the meantime, the espresso you make while learning will suck. You will go through enough milk to feed a small island nation while learning how to steam milk.

But even if you have the spare cash for a good machine, *and* the spare time to learn how to use it, here are some other reasons to help you reconsider buying an espresso machine:

> They're very messy;

> Yet you have to keep them spotless to make nice drinks;

> Yet they are a massive pain in the ass to clean;

> They take up a *lot* of counter space;

> And quality grinders take up even more counter space;

> They're very noisy;

> When you invite friends around for coffee, you will have to make each espresso drink individually, which takes ages, and you will have to do it while yelling over your noisy machine, and then you will have to clean up all the mess you made, which takes even longer, and in the end your friends will be underwhelmed by your amateur attempt at a latte that is nowhere near as good as the one they could have just bought down the street in half the time.

Once you have mastered several other brewing methods, you can dial in your stepless grinder like a pro, and can identify a Jamaica Blue Mountain from an Ethiopian Harar in a blind tasting, *then* if you are still dreaming of making espresso at home, go ahead and spend several months' salary on a shiny prosumer machine. Until that point, I strongly advise that you direct your time and dollars elsewhere.

So now that that's out of the way, let's break down some more realistic options, and weigh the pros and cons of each.

METHOD, MAN

The difference between coffee-making methods and actual coffee equipment can get really confusing. What we call a "pour-over brewer" employs the pour-over method, and an espresso machine employs the espresso method, but a French press employs . . . the immersion method? Let's break it down.

IMMERSION: This is where the coffee grounds are fully immersed (or steeped) in water for some length of time. Because the water typically spends more time absorbing the flavors of the coffee, this method tends to produce a richer, fuller-bodied cup.

EXAMPLES: French press, siphon, Toddy.

POUR-OVER/DRIP: In these methods, hot water is poured over the grounds, saturating them, and then passes through a filter and drips out below. The term "drip" includes your standard household electric brewers, so we tend to use the term "pour-over" or "manual pour-over" when discussing human-powered brewers that require you to physically pour the water over the coffee yourself. Pour-over coffees tend to produce cleaner, lighter-bodied cups.

EXAMPLES: Chemex, Hario V60, Melitta.

ESPRESSO: Because the United States is relatively new to espresso, many people refer to it as a distinct entity from "coffee." Stop doing that. Espresso is simply another method of making coffee.

FRENCH PRESS

The French have traditionally made and enjoyed terrible coffee, and that practice continues largely unabated today (though there are a handful of very good coffee shops in Paris now). Still, they did give the world this—kinda. The first patent for a French press–like coffee brewer was indeed filed by a couple of

Frenchmen in 1850s, though its invention is often credited to an Italian designer, whose 1920s patent is closer to the product we use today.

But we'll give this one to the French, because the method hasn't changed all that much over the years: you dump some grounds in the bottom of a glass pot, fill it with hot water, wait a few minutes, then plunge the metal filter down; the grounds are pushed to the bottom, and the coffee is forced to the top. The resulting drink is rich and robust, but also a little oily.

The contraption has been popular in Europe for decades but, like EDM, only became big in the United States. in the '90s. In most high-end coffee shops, however, it has since been usurped by electric drip brewers for large batches, and pour-over styles for made-to-order drinks.

PROS: The French press is cheap, quick, and simple, and allows you to make several cups of coffee at once, which is particularly useful for the workplace. More importantly, it's large and attractive enough that you can justify leaving one sitting on your desk, making you look très European.

CONS: The porous filter means sediment often sneaks into your drink, leaving it grittier than a Ken Loach film.

AVERAGE COST: A decent press from Danish company Bodum starts at around $30. You can go cheaper, but you don't want to—the crappier the filter, the dirtier that cup is going to get. You will also need something to decant the coffee into immediately after brewing, but as discussed earlier in the chapter, you might already have something appropriate lying around the house.

DEGREE OF DIFFICULTY: Very low.

COFFEE CRED: If you want to pinpoint the exact moment where the French press jumped the shark, look no further than July 20, 2004, when Ted Allen recommended it to a sixty-six-year-old man on an episode of *Queer Eye for the Straight Guy*. It's definitely a solid and respected brewing method, but you're not going to impress anyone.

POUR-OVER

The original pour-over coffee maker was invented by a German housewife in 1908. This probably explains why your grandma has one, too. Don't let that turn you off though—the method has seen a massive rise in popularity and trendiness since the late 2000s—partially thanks to a Japanese pour-over brewer, the Hario V60, hitting the U.S. market and becoming a big hit with baristas, and partially thanks to the re-emergence of the American-made Chemex (see following). There are a bunch of other Japanese brands out there—Bee House, Bonmac, Kalita—(and also some non-Japanese ones) all with slightly different designs and materials. They all largely employ the same method, though: you place a paper (or sometimes metal) filter and grounds into the cone-shaped brewer, and slowly pour in hot water on top; the water passes through the grounds, extracting the flavor, and drips through the filter and into a cup below. The final product is clean, flavorful, and aromatic—so long as you do it correctly.

PROS: A relatively inexpensive way to geek out with brewing. The amount of control you have means you can really play around with adjusting variables like filter size, grind, and pouring speed to get the best out of your beans. Also, the various products are cheap enough that you can collect them all, then impress your friends with lines like: "Everyone knows the V60, but you can buy those at Crate & Barrel these days. I have to import my Kalita Wave filters in from Yokohama, but it's worth it—the extraction is much more even."

CONS: Lots of variables means lots of things can go wrong. Though they look quite simple, some of the brewers are deceptively tricky to master, requiring lots of practice to nail down the right pouring speed and pattern.

AVERAGE COST: The brewers themselves are pretty cheap— starting at $4 for a plastic Melitta and going up to $20 for a glass or ceramic V60—while a pack of paper filters is about $4 (except Kalita Wave filters, which are about $13 a pack). But you definitely, definitely should invest in a gooseneck kettle for this method, and that will probably be the most expensive pour-over-related purchase. There are lots of other pour-over accessories on the market these days—stands, decanters, metal filters—but these are all totally optional extras.

DEGREE OF DIFFICULTY: Medium to hard, depending on the brewer.

COFFEE CRED: Very solid. Of course, the more obscure and Japanese your model is, the more impressive—maybe those pricey Kalita filters are worth the extra dollars, after all.

CHEMEX

This is also technically a manual pour-over brewer—and the final product isn't all that different—but, as in real life, the Chemex coffeemaker deserves special treatment because it is much more physically attractive. Instead of a dripper you place over your cup, the Chemex is a single unit—a big glass decanter with an hourglass figure that allows a filter to sit in the top, while the coffee drips down into the bottom chamber. The brewer has ridden a similar recent surge in popularity, as have its more homely little pour-over cousins, but it has long been an icon of Bauhaus-style design and functionality. Created by a U.S.-based German inventor in 1941, the Chemex has been a fixture in New York's Museum of Modern Art since 1944, and was used by James Bond in *From Russia with Love*.

PROS: Unless your Nespresso machine actually came with George Clooney or Penelope Cruz attached, this is about as sexy as coffeemakers get. Seriously, even if you never figure out how to use it, the Chemex has great ornamental value. And assuming you *do* figure out how to use it, it can be a little easier to manage and master than many other pour-overs. It makes an extremely clean cup, thanks to thicker paper filters, and the larger models also allow you to make several cups at once. Pulling out a Chemex at the end of your dinner party and preparing some tableside is a surefire way to thrill (okay, mildly impress) your guests, both with the crowd-pleasing brew and your stylish taste in design.

CONS: It is a time-suck. As with other pour-overs, you have to hover over the brewer, dripping in water, ever . . . so . . . slowly . . . and . . . precisely. It is also way too breakable and complicated for travel or work.

DEGREE OF DIFFICULTY: Medium, with a bit of practice.

AVERAGE COST: Glass-handled 8-cup brewers start at about $40, and go up to about $95 for a 32-cup with a handsome '70s-chic wood and leather collar around the middle. Filter packs are about $7.50, though reusable stainless-steel filters are now available for $60. You will also definitely want a gooseneck kettle for this guy.

COFFEE CRED: Super high. We are probably at peak Chemex right now.

AEROPRESS

The AeroPress was created in 2005 by inventor and Stanford University engineering lecturer Alan Adler—perhaps better known as the creator of the Aerobie flying disc, which is perhaps better known as "that Frisbee-looking thing shaped like a ring." Much like the Aerobie, the Aeropress is made of plastic and works really fast. You put a small paper filter, some coffee grounds, and hot water into the plastic tube, then put a second, smaller tube inside and push down like a syringe. It is generally considered to be an immersion brewer, but the actual immersion time is very short. The air between the two tubes pushes the coffee through the filter and into your cup, and sixty seconds later, you have a rich, incredibly smooth cup of coffee.

PROS: Fast, cheap, easy to clean, durable, portable, delicious.

CONS: The brewing technique lacks the style and elegance of a pour-over, and there is less room for experimentation. Only makes one or two cups at a time. It kind of looks like a male enhancement pump.

DEGREE OF DIFFICULTY: Low.

AVERAGE COST: $26 for the AeroPress and about $3 for a pack of filters. Several companies also now offer reusable metal Aeropress filters for between $10 and $18. They're by no means a necessity, but they are great for travel, and provide a little more diversity in your AeroPress-ing, with different models affecting the drink in different ways. The metal also allows more oils through than a paper filter, resulting in a more full-bodied and flavorful cup.

COFFEE CRED: The AeroPress isn't much to look at, and it is still growing in recognition stateside, but if you want to get in on the ground floor of a coffee trend, this is an ideal place to place your chips. The device is already huge in Scandinavia, which is pretty much at the forefront of global coffee trends, and AeroPress coffee-making competitions are becoming an increasingly important part of the competitive coffee circuit (yes, there is such a thing).

CLEVER COFFEE DRIPPER

The plastic Clever Coffee Dripper, made by a Taiwanese company called Absolutely Best Idea Development (gotta love that level of confidence; you will also sometimes see this device referred to as an "Abid"), looks a lot like other pour-over brewers, but it is a very different beast—a Frankenstein creation, even. You put in a paper filter and coffee grounds and fill with hot water, same as usual, but the brewer has a stopper at the bottom, so the water doesn't start dripping out until you want it to. That means the coffee can sit and steep for a few minutes, turning it into a hybrid between an immersion and pour-over brewer. The result is a cup that has the body and flavor of, say, a French press, with the clarity of a Chemex, because none of the gross sediment gets through the paper. The stopper also means you don't have to pour in the water slowly or carefully—a boon for both the uncoordinated and the lazy.

Another company called Bonavita recently created a very similar competitor dubbed the Immersion Dripper, which is made from porcelain.

PROS: All the trendiness of a pour-over for people who secretly don't like the taste or hassle of pour-over. You also don't need a fancy kettle, which makes it an excellent option for the workplace.

CONS: It might sound like a great option when traveling, but the Clever is not known for its durability. They can't go in the dishwasher, and don't always last long.

DEGREE OF DIFFICULTY: Low. It's a little more involved than a French press because of the paper filter, but worth the extra effort.

AVERAGE COST: About $18 to $22, depending on which size model you get, plus about $5 for a box of filters. The Bonavita Immersion Dripper costs about $40.

COFFEE CRED: The Clever definitely earns bonus points for obscurity. People will say, "Is that a pour-over?" and you can sound all knowledgeable replying, "No, it's this brewer I got from Taiwan—" (you can get them in the United States, but technically it is not a lie, because that is where they are manufactured) and then nonchalantly drop a little knowledge about the differences between immersion and pour-over brewing. On the other hand, it's clunkier and less stylish than most actual pour-over brewers—like orthopedic sneakers, it makes life easier and appears close to the original, but it has an unmistakably dorky air of practicality about it.

SIPHON

As covered in the last chapter, the siphon or vac pot has recently become a popular staple in trendy U.S. coffee shops, but it actually has a long history as a home brewer—particularly in Europe, but even here in the United States.

The first-known patent for a siphon brewer was filed in Germany in the 1830s, but the first commercially successful version was created by a French woman in 1840. Americans by and large continued to brew their coffee like philistines for the next seventy years, until around 1910, when a pair of sisters from Massachusetts patented a version called the "Silex." Many Americans did buy Silexes and subsequent other American-designed siphon brewers, and continued to do so until about the middle of the century, when simpler, faster (and mostly shittier) methods took over.

Surprisingly, siphon coffee then took off in Japan, both in cafés and at home. And over there, it stuck around. There are now Japanese coffee shops that only serve siphon coffee and the country even hosts a World Siphonist Championship.

As a result, many of the coolest siphon brewers are now made by Japanese companies, like Hario and Yama, though Danish manufacturer Bodum and the UK's Cona also make popular models.

PROS: The brewers themselves look awesome, but the brewing looks even better. When the coffee suddenly whooshes up to the top chamber, you will feel *and* look like a wizard.

CONS: The method is fairly hands-on and time-consuming, while the brewer itself is highly breakable. There is a very real chance of burning yourself on either the glass or the burner—many people actually use gloves or heat pads while using them. Not advisable before midday—it's never a great idea to fiddle around with naked flames before you've had your morning coffee. Not portable.

DEGREE OF DIFFICULTY: High.

AVERAGE COST: The stovetop models are around $35 to $55, while the ones with inbuilt burners run anywhere from $55 to $300. You will also need a thermometer.

COFFEE CRED: High. If you can nail the brewing method, you will wow anyone who steps foot in your home (except maybe Mormons).

MOKA POT

After the Vespa scooter, the Olivetti typewriter, and Fabio's abs, the moka pot is probably one of the most successful marriages of Italian form and function. Created in the 1930s, today pretty much every Italian kitchen has one (or more), as do many in Latin America.

Although they are sometimes referred to as stovetop espresso makers, moka pots do not technically make espresso. They do, however, work in a similar fashion: forcing pressurized water through ground coffee. Only upward, instead of downward, and with far less pressure than an actual espresso machine.

Cheap, low-tech, and stylish (today you will find them in many modern art museums), it's easy to see why they caught on so well in their espresso-mad native land, especially during the Depression. The drink might not have *quite* been espresso, but it wasn't so far off, and a moka pot at home was probably far more accessible than visiting trendy espresso bars for much of the country.

The little metal pots are comprised of two chambers with a filter basket between them. The bottom chamber is filled with water, and the basket is packed with grounds. As the water heats up, the steam forces the water up through a funnel and into the basket. It then pushes through to the top chamber, bubbling out into a thick and potent brew.

PROS: Timeless style. Fairly hands-off for a manual brewing method.

CONS: The final product can be a bit sludgy and is often over-extracted because it is so easy to overheat. If you don't make it correctly, the pot can spit out boiling hot coffee at you like a pissed-off llama.

DEGREE OF DIFFICULTY: Theoretically easy, but it's also easy to screw it up.

AVERAGE COST: From $15 for a little aluminum pot up to around $50 for a large, slick stainless-steel model. There are also some *super*-fancy ones for $100 and above, but you really don't need to spend that much unless you want to, for their aesthetic value.

COFFEE CRED: The moka is still a fairly schismatic brewing device in the trendy coffee world—it *can* make a very nice cup of coffee, but it often doesn't, so many would rather use something else. Let's say the odds are fifty-fifty someone will raise a mildly impressed eyebrow at your moka mastery.

MO' MOCHA MO' PROBLEMS

⊘ ⊘ ⊘

Ordering a "café moka" in Italy will get you a cup of coffee brewed in a moka pot, while ordering a "café mocha" in the United States will get you some sort of chocolaty crap (see Chapter 4). Though unrelated, both were actually named for the Yemeni port city of Mocha, which was a major coffee marketplace back in the day.

Then there is the mocha varietal of the coffee plant (sometimes mokha, moka, or mocca), which presumably hails from Yemen, but is now grown elsewhere as well.

Further confusing the matter is "Mocha-Java" coffee. The O.G. coffee blend, it was first created by combining actual Yemen Mocha and Indonesian Java coffees. The name has stuck around, but these days the Mocha part is typically substituted with Ethiopian coffee (Yemen still produces a bit of coffee, but doesn't export much), and the Java component sometimes comes from elsewhere in Indonesia.

TURKISH COFFEE

Real talk: Turkish coffee, Cypriot coffee, Greek coffee, Egyptian coffee, Lebanese coffee . . . it's all basically the same thing. Just don't say that in any of those countries. Sure, there are slight regional differences in preparation and serving, but the thick brew that caps off your meal at sundry Middle Eastern, North African, and some Mediterranean restaurants is usually fundamentally the same—and has been for several centuries.

The coffee is prepared in a little brass or copper pot called an *ibrik, briki,* or *cezve,* depending on whom you're speaking to. The pot is heated multiple times on a stove until the coffee forms a thick froth on top, then its contents are poured into a small cup about the size of a demitasse. It is often also brewed with sugar (lots and lots of sugar) and sometimes also with ground cardamom or other spices.

You don't hear a lot about Turkish coffee in the contemporary coffee world, but it can actually be a really pleasant alternative to an espresso when made with good-quality, freshly ground beans. It's rich and strong, though often also a little gritty because it is not filtered.

PROS: Fairly simple to make. Some of the painted ibriks are really gorgeous. When accompanied by home-brewed Turkish coffee, eating kebabs and smoking hookah seems like a legitimate cultural activity instead of just an unhealthy Saturday night in.

CONS: Unless you know someone who can read coffee grounds, they will probably spoil the last few sips of your drink.

DEGREE OF DIFFICULTY: The actual method is quite easy, but it requires a lot of concentration because if the coffee reaches a boil, it's ruined.

AVERAGE COST: Small, plain ibriks start at about $13 and can go up to $60 for large, beautifully engraved or painted models. But you will also need a good grinder capable of a very fine grind. You can buy specialty Turkish hand grinders online for about $60.

COFFEE CRED: Minimal. Your hippie uncle—the one who backpacked through the Middle East in the '60s—will probably be impressed, but this preparation method has never really been anointed cool by the coffee cognoscenti.

EVA SOLO CAFÉ SOLO

The what? Yeah, you've probably never even heard of this immersion brewer, which is a shame because it makes a nice cup of coffee and is pretty sexy, to boot. The Café Solo was created by Danish company Eva Solo (and is often just referred to as an Eva Solo in the United States) about ten years ago, and has definitely earned many fans since, but seems to have dropped off the radar a bit of late.

The device itself is a glass carafe with a mesh filter that sits in the neck, and a Neoprene case (Neoprene is that stuff wetsuits and laptop cases are made from) that zips up around it. It kind of looks like it is wearing a North Face jacket, but the case is actually there to keep the temperature hot and stable, not to make it look like a douche. The coffee steeps in the bottom of the carafe, before being poured out through the filter at the top. The resulting cup is similar to that of a French press, but cleaner.

PROS: Simple to use, looks cool, offers a great alternative to the French press. If you don't want to scare your non-coffee-nerd friends by whipping out your full pour-over rig after dinner, this is a more understated way to show off.

CONS: Expensive—it's better than a French press, but is it $50 better?

AVERAGE COST: About $80 online, maybe a little more or less, depending on where you find one.

DEGREE OF DIFFICULTY: Very low.

COFFEE CRED: Medium. This brewer isn't quite as buzzy as it has been, but it's definitely well regarded by those in the know.

Plus, it's Danish. The Danes invented Lego and Lars von Trier—they make cool things.

SINGLE-SERVE COFFEE MACHINES

It seems unlikely you would be reading a book called *Coffee Nerd* if you were even considering buying one of these things, but they are currently taking the world by storm, so they probably deserve a mention just in case. If nothing else, you should understand what they are so when your workplace inevitably buys one, you can smugly explain why your coffee-making method is both ethically and gustatorily superior.

Nespresso, Keurig, Senseo, whatever brand you're familiar with, they all work pretty much the same way: you stick a pod or packet or capsule of pre-ground coffee inside a machine, press a button, and out comes some very mediocre espresso. Some of the higher-end models also have milk steamers and other bells and whistles.

PROS: The appeal of the single-serve machine is basically all the arguments I made for not buying an espresso machine (minus the part where you decide to continue buying espresso in cafés, instead of settling for this subpar version at home). Though they typically cost *at least* $100, that is still far cheaper than the real thing, and you don't have to have any skills or training to operate one. The packets themselves cost about seventy-five cents to $1, which, again, is not cheap for something you make at home, but is cheaper than a $4 store-bought latte. Though they only produce very mediocre espresso, most of the better brands never produce woefully awful espresso, either, which is a pretty big selling point for many people who drink mediocre espresso anyway.

The machines have also become popular in many restaurants, where even mediocre espresso is a step up from what most waiters can produce, and this may be the only scenario in which they are defensible.

CONS: Aside from the mediocre coffee and poor-quality, old, pre-ground beans (and do you need anything else?), these things are incredibly wasteful. Do you really want to churn through that much plastic *every* time you make a coffee? Think of the poor baby whales.

DEGREE OF DIFFICULTY: A four-year-old could do it.

AVERAGE COST: Anywhere from $70 to $250, plus your dignity.

COFFEE CRED: Zero. Less than zero, even. Negative bajillion.

COLD BREW

Unless you live in Florida, you probably don't want to drink cold brew all year round, and certainly not as your primary coffee beverage. But it is absolutely worth dabbling in at home, because let's be honest—even the nerdiest coffee nerd doesn't *always* feel like grinding and measuring and faffing about every time they want a nice cup of coffee. To make a nice cup of cold brew, you just have to pre-prepare a batch once a week, then take the concentrate out of your fridge whenever you get the urge and literally just add water (or don't; a straight shot of concentrate in the morning is a hell of an eye-opener).

By far the best-known cold brew brewer on the U.S. market is the Toddy—to the point that many people now refer to cold brew coffee simply as "Toddy coffee," regardless of how it is made. The brewer was actually invented by an American named Todd Simpson (yes, he named it after himself in the oddest way) back in 1964, but its popularity here is pretty recent. The other product you will see around a lot is the Filtron, which is very similar.

PROS: Dead simple—even the brewing method is pretty much set and forget. One batch can last all week. Highly portable—take a big batch of it on a picnic, or make a giant drink in a recycled Big Gulp cup and take it with you to go. If you're willing to pay for a Kyoto drip tower (Yama makes 29-inch models, and Hario, 18-inch ones, that are perhaps more appropriate for the home than the giant versions you see in cafés), they will transform even the crappiest microwave-and-toaster-oven kitchen into a paragon of style.

CONS: It's cold.

DEGREE OF DIFFICULTY: You will have to experiment a little to get the water-to-grounds ratio right, but otherwise low.

AVERAGE COST: You can make your own out of a Mason jar and a cheese cloth, but a Filtron or Toddy will set you back about $40. Both the smaller Yama and Hario towers are around $250 (try to think of them as cheap art rather than expensive coffeemakers). An eBay search will also yield a huge range of weird and wonderful Japanese and South Korean cold brew makers not otherwise available in the United States. (My favorite is a Korean one named "Juliet's Tears" from a company called Café Romeo; I have no idea if it's any good, I'm just perplexed at the idea of naming a product after the grief of a suicidal teenager. A little taste of tragedy in every cup!)

COFFEE CRED: High. Cold brew coffee is so hot right now (in a manner of speaking), and it is so simple, you can easily impress guests by whipping up café-quality cold brew at home. Bringing a big pitcher to picnics and barbecues should also win friends and influence people.

Experimental Brewers

Buoyed by the growing number of coffee nerds and the growing popularity of crowdfunding, there has recently been a surge in upstart inventors creating new coffee brewers and funding them online through pre-sales and contributions from geeks eager to get their hands on the next big thing. Some are totally original creations, others just new takes or alleged "improvements" on more traditional brewers.

How can you tell if the product will be any good? It's a total crapshoot. You can always take a look at the pedigree of the inventor—do they work in the coffee industry, or are they just some home tinkerer?—but bear in mind that the Melitta, the Chemex, the AeroPress, and the Toddy were not invented by coffee professionals.

PROS: You *could* score yourself the next hottest thing in the coffee world and bragging rights.

CONS: You could score yourself a really expensive hunk of plastic or glass.

DEGREE OF DIFFICULTY: If you're backing a completely untested product on Kickstarter, chances are you're going to get a beta model. There likely will be kinks to be worked out, and you are basically signing up (and paying) to be a guinea pig. There won't be a lot of help or advice available from anyone but the product's creator, so you will probably have to muddle your way through the brewing process alone. This doesn't necessarily mean it will be *hard*, but you probably don't want to make this your first brewer.

AVERAGE COST: It varies, of course. On the one hand, pre-sale and crowdfunded products are usually considerably cheaper than they will be if and when they hit the market for real. On the other, they are likely to still be pretty pricey because the manufacturers producing them won't have the tools in place to automate the process.

COFFEE CRED: Potentially pretty high—even if the brewer ends up being a total dud, it'll probably be so obscure no one else who sees it at your house will know that. If they ask to try some, you can just say, "You know, this product is still in an experimental phase—this is one of the only models in the world—and I haven't *quite* perfected it yet."

Coffee on the Go

One of the huge downsides to discovering the pleasures of high-quality coffee is that you won't be able to go back to the cheap swill you were imbibing before. Nor should you! But what about when you're at work? Or traveling?

You probably won't be able to replicate your ideal coffee-making setup in either of these circumstances, but it doesn't mean you have to settle for vending machine coffee or hotel room coffeemakers, either.

For the Workplace

A handgrinder is likely your best bet here, unless you can somehow convince your boss to buy a burr grinder (so basically, you work in Silicon Valley or you yourself are the boss because, come on, no one else is going to indulge this kind of outrageous request). Another option is to grind your morning coffee before leaving the house and bringing it to work in a zip-top bag—it's not ideal, but it's better than nothing. Brewers that don't require slow, careful water pouring are going to be the most suitable (unless you really want to bring your own kettle to work, and even I think that's taking it a bit far), so: AeroPress, Clever, or French press. The advisability of purchasing a scale for your place of work is directly proportionate to how much you think your workmates will mock you for doing so. It *could* be the thing that tips their perception of your obsessive coffee-making regime from "Wow, Gary must have such a refined palate!" to "Wow, Gary is f***ing nuts!"

For Travel

This is a little more difficult, but bringing your own gear affords you the opportunity to sample local roasters wherever you are headed—which can be especially fun in other countries (and which is just as well, because trying to sneak coffee past most airport customs officers is a really bad idea). An AeroPress with a reusable metal filter is really unbeatable here because it hardly takes up any room in your luggage and is much easier to clean than any other brewer. Pair it with a lightweight hand grinder (on this occasion, you should probably forgo a scale), and you'll be laughing while your travel companions are all choking down crappy fast food coffee to stay awake.

Further Reading

> Coffee Geek (*www.coffeegeek.com*) is a popular website and forum for, well, you know who, with product reviews and guides from both professionals and consumers.

> Seattle Coffee Gear (*www.seattlecoffeegear.com*) is a Washington-based chain of stores and online retailer that sells a large range of equipment for both amateurs and pros. Even if you're not buying its products, the staff members make great videos of themselves testing out just about every item in their catalog, and they're not afraid to identify and criticize any problems they find. It is a great way to see products in action before you buy them.

> Prima Coffee Equipment (*www.prima-coffee.com*) is another equipment retailer that has videos. Its ones tend to be more "Hey, look at this awesome product!" but it is still useful to see the gear doing its thing. The company also has a great blog, with brewing guides and product comparisons.

SIX

Buy Some Coffee Beans

Even with the best grinder and coffeemaker in the world, you simply cannot make good coffee with shitty beans.

If you're already hanging out at great coffee shops, getting access to the good stuff seems like it shouldn't be that hard. You give them a painfully large percentage of your disposable income, and they exchange it for a mind-blowing product, right? Well, maybe. Even at the coolest café in town, you need to know what to look for, or you could still end up with a bag of really expensive compost.

And even once you secure the goods, you might still wind up with shitty coffee if you don't know how to take care of it. So let's break down where to shop, what to look for once you're there, and how to proceed once you get home.

Where's the Bean?

In this post-Amazon Prime world, spending more than five minutes shopping for *anything* seems like a ludicrous hassle. But if you want to get your hands on the best beans around, you're going to have to do some research and possibly even—gasp—leave the house. Assuming you found a sufficiently trendy third-wave coffee shop back in Chapter 4, you already know of at least one trendy third-wave roaster: whatever they're using. And certainly, that brand would seem like a pretty good option for your first batch. But that café *might* not be the optimal place to buy them—as you'll see, baristas don't often make the best retailers. So here are your best options for finding great coffee, in order of (my) preference for them.

ROASTER-RUN COFFEE SHOPS

There are actually two types of trendy third-wave coffee shops—the ones that are run by coffee roasters and the ones that aren't. The former is basically your best-case scenario as a buyer—these guys will have the freshest product and give great recommendations on what to buy and how to prepare it, and you may even be buying from the person who roasted the coffee himself. They will also often sell their product in smaller quantities than you will find elsewhere, which is really handy if you're just buying for yourself.

NON-ROASTING COFFEE SHOPS

Cafés that aren't part of a roasting business—i.e., they buy their beans in from a roaster—*might* offer a similar experience, but they are less of a sure thing. They will almost certainly sell whole beans from whichever roaster(s) they use as well. However, their staff might be less knowledgeable about the product, they will probably only retail larger volumes, and what they have in stock won't necessarily be that fresh—I've been to plenty of otherwise first-rate cafés and found some seriously dusty bags on their shelves. This is potentially still an excellent option, just be diligent and check the roast date (see later in this chapter) for how long they've been sitting around.

ONLINE

Many roasters also sell their beans through their websites, and this can also be a great option. Take a look at their shipping policies—good ones will mail them shortly after they were roasted, which (assuming you live near civilization) will still get them to you pretty fresh. Many smaller roasters only roast and ship once a week, and this is actually a good sign—it means they really give a shit about freshness and quality and making sure people consume their product at its best. One downside here is that you don't have a barista or server to help you make a choice. Another is that most roasters don't sell very small quantities online, so make sure you check just how much coffee you're committing to before you click "add to cart." Some roasters also offer "subscriptions"—meaning they mail out a new shipment at regular intervals—which is good if you're forgetful, but not so much if your coffee consumption is erratic.

There are also now a number of third-party subscription services that send you a box with small tasters of different roasters at regular intervals. This could be a neat way to discover and sample some of the best roasters from around the country (there are some really good ones involved), but they don't usually come cheap and there is definitely an ethical and environmental argument to be made for supporting local roasters if you can.

GROCERY STORES

You *can* buy beans from grocery stores, but definitely not the kind of grocery stores that put coupons in your mailbox for half-off sirloin and buy-one-get-one frozen waffles. You might be able to buy good beans at your local hippy co-op (the one that smells like lavender oil and has a community notice board advertising Wiccan covens and nude yoga groups), though those places tend to prioritize features like organic and fair trade over quality and freshness.

Really, what you're looking for is one of those small, super-fancy boutique grocery stores that sell really expensive cheese and artisanal peanut butter. Those places often also stock coffee from good local roasters. But even then, you have to examine the package carefully to make sure it's actually fresh, because it very frequently won't be. For instance, my local grocery store offers a fantastic array of great roasters, but when I check the label, the beans have often been roasted over a month ago. I'm sure it doesn't make good economic sense for them to rotate their stock as frequently as coffee requires, but that is their problem. This is definitely my least-preferred option for this reason. If you *must* do it, try to get to the stock farthest back on the shelf, which should be the freshest. Yes, this is a jerk move, but what can you do?

FARMERS' MARKETS

This is a bit of a wildcard option. It is not unusual for upstart micro-roasters to start out flogging their wares at farmers' markets. Even if their coffees aren't *quite* the greatest yet, this is a pretty awesome opportunity to chat firsthand with a pro (well, semi-pro) roaster and grill them for all the gritty details about where their coffee is from, what they're doing to it, and how you should brew it. Buy some of their stuff, then come back the following week to discuss it.

Obviously you can't *count* on this option—not everyone lives near a farmers' market, not every farmers' market has a coffee vendor, let alone a good one, and the markets are seasonal—but if all these things work out in your favor, definitely try it out at least once.

Know Your Product

Some roasters' packaging has all the detail of a Mark Rothko painting, minimalist and mystifying, while others' better resemble a NASCAR driver's uniform, plastered with logos and certifications. You want to walk out of your preferred coffee retailer with something you're going to love, but you also don't want to sound like a total moron at the counter saying, "Er, I'll have the 'Fazenda,' thanks." (That's Portuguese for "farm" and the one word you could pick from the label of a Brazilian coffee that will tell the salesperson absolutely nothing). So what does it all mean?

WHAT'S IN A NAME?

Oh for the days when coffees were named things like "Morning Sunshine" and "Midnight Express." As of this writing, Stumptown Coffee Roasters has something for sale called "Guatemala Finca El Injerto - Bourbon"—perhaps not the most accessible title for a coffee newcomer. But don't be put off—this one is actually pretty simple if you can parse it out. "Guatemala" is . . . Guatemala. "Finca" is Spanish for "estate," so "Finca El Injerto" is the name of the estate (farm, basically) it comes from. And if you read Chapter 3, you know that Bourbon is a varietal of the coffee plant (sorry, there is no booze in these beans). Here is one from Blue Bottle Coffee: "Ethiopia Yirgacheffe Gelena Abaya Washed." You know Ethiopia, and by now, you probably know that Yirgacheffe is a famous coffee-growing region in Ethiopia. You probably don't know that Gelena Abaya is a subregion of

Yirgacheffe (hey, I had to Google it, too), but you can probably guess that it is either that or the name of a farm, estate, or cooperative. And, again, if you read Chapter 3, you know that "washed" refers to the way the beans have been processed. But don't sweat it too much since no one expects you to have an encyclopedic knowledge of farm names and tiny subregions within subregions, anyway. Just focus on the bits you do know, and Google the rest later.

TL;DR: Roasters often label their coffees with very long, incomprehensible titles. Don't let it intimidate you.

THE FINE PRINT

Regardless of what the coffee is called, some labels will also list details like the country and region of origin, processing method, elevation (or altitude, same thing), varietal, and some basic tasting notes. You might want to go back and learn all about these things in Chapter 3 so they actually mean something to you.

ROAST DATE

On most food products, it is important to check the expiration date. Not coffee. Coffee doesn't technically expire for a long time, but that doesn't mean it is still worth drinking.

Roasted coffee actually has an extremely short shelf life between the points of "excellent" and "meh," and the clock starts ticking down from the moment it is roasted. The quality starts to drop seriously about ten days out, so ideally, you want to consume it within about two weeks from when it is roasted. It's not going to be *bad* at five weeks out, per se, it's just going to get dull. And life is too short for dull coffee—especially when you're paying a premium price.

That is why the most important date on a bag of coffee—some of the most important information on a bag of coffee period—is the bit that says "roasted on." Once you start looking for this, you will probably be pretty shocked at how many grocery stores and coffee shops are selling beans that are *months* old. And if the roaster doesn't label its bags with the roasting date at all, this is not the roaster you are looking for.

FAIR TRADE

Most people are familiar with the term "fair trade" and have a vague notion that it is a nice thing to do, but few actually understand what it specifically entails.

This is as simply as I can put it: To qualify for a certification from Fair Trade USA (green circle logo) or Fairtrade International (green and blue circle logo), growers need to meet certain ethical and environmental standards—no child labor, no GMOs, democratic decision-making processes, safe working conditions, to name a few. And in return, buyers must pay a minimum price for their coffee and also provide some extra money that goes back into community and farm development. The important thing to know about fair trade certifications is that they are not necessarily a marker of better *coffee*—just coffee produced under conditions that meet a certain standard, with the goal of improving life for workers and their communities.

Historically, both Fair Trade USA and Fairtrade International have only certified cooperatives of growers, not individual farms. This is one reason many third-wave roasters don't purchase fair trade beans—they find it easier to source really high-quality stuff from individual farms than from large groups of farms. Fair Trade USA is now running pilot programs to cover small farms as well as workers on bigger estates, but it'll be a while before that rolls out globally.

CUP OF EXCELLENCE

The Cup of Excellence sounds like the title of a cheap Harry Potter knockoff, but is actually a series of coffee competitions. The contest was started in 1999 by a bunch of specialty coffee folk, and is held mostly annually in some South American, Central American, and African growing countries.

The way it works is roughly like this: Any farm can submit their beans to their country's competition. The beans are roasted and cupped by a panel of local tasters, who score them out of 100. They go through three rounds of cupping, whittling them down to the top sixty that have scored over eighty-five. Then, a jury of tasters from around the world comes in and performs three more rounds of cupping, whittling the coffees down to the top ten.

But the *real* prize comes when the organization auctions off the top coffees online. Buyers and roasters from around the world bid big for the best beans, and the producers keep most of the money. The winning Guatemalan lot in 2014 went for $42.40 a pound; the winning Honduran one went for $35.10 a pound. By contrast, the current market price for arabica beans, as of writing, is about $1.80 a pound.

Not part of the Cup of Excellence, but very similar, is the Best of Panama (remember those super-pricey geshas mentioned in Chapter 3? The 2014 Best of Panama winner went for $107.86 a pound).

Anyway, sometimes roasters will note a Cup of Excellence winner on the label.

COFFEE REVIEW SCORES

Coffee Review (*www.coffeereview.com*) is an established website that does exactly what it says. This is not the Yelp of coffee —the site is run by veteran cupper and coffee writer Kenneth Davids, and assesses dozens of coffees every month, offering tasting notes and scoring each on a 100-point rating system. If their coffees receive high marks (generally over ninety), some roasters will label them with the site's logo and the score.

DIRECT TRADE

As discussed in Chapter 2, "direct trade" is an unregulated term that means different things to different people. For the purists, "direct trade" means that the roaster purchased the coffee *directly* from the grower for a price negotiated directly with them—ideally as part of an ongoing relationship between the two. But others might buy from a farm they've never stepped foot on through a third party, and still stamp the term "direct trade" on their packaging. There's nothing stopping them.

If you want to know more about what particular roasters mean when they use the term, a good place to start would be to check out their websites. Many will outline how they source and buy their coffee in great detail—some have a list of principles, others do annual reports, a few even divulge the actual prices they paid to producers. If a roaster's green-coffee buyer is regularly visiting and interacting with farms and co-ops "at origin," as they say, they might be blogging the whole thing in great detail, too. Or again, just contact them.

Meanwhile, if a coffee isn't labeled as "direct trade" or something similar, it doesn't *necessarily* mean that the roaster hasn't done its due diligence, or that they didn't pay a fair price, or that anything suspicious is going on. Plenty of great roasters get their beans via reliable importers and exporters who do ensure fair prices and good farming practices. Or the coffee might have been purchased via auction. Or maybe they just don't like the term.

ORGANIC

A coffee label bearing that now-familiar "USDA Organic" logo or even just the word "organic" means that both the farm that grew at least 95 percent of the beans and the roaster that roasted them and anyone else who handled them in between (like an importer, or a decaffeination plant) have been certified organic. So it is more than just not spraying the coffee plants with nasty chemicals—equipment and storage facilities have to pass muster, too.

If buying and consuming organic products is important to you for health or environmental reasons or because you think it will impress your yuppie friends, then it is certainly something to look out for. But be aware that a lot of coffee comes from farms that are unofficially organic because that's just the way they roll in a lot of countries. Getting certified costs money and time, which plenty of farms can't spare.

BIRD FRIENDLY

Not to kill your buzz or anything, but a lot of the coffee you have consumed in your life was grown at a serious cost to the environment. Coffee plants like being in the sun, but birds and other adorable (and even not-so-adorable-but-still-very-important) creatures kind of like having trees and grass to hang out in. So the Smithsonian Migratory Bird Center offers a "Bird

Friendly" certification to farms that maintain nice habitats for migratory birds (and, again, other wildlife, but the Migratory Bird Center is pretty big on migratory birds). It is not so easy to get. Snagging that designation means your farm has to be certified organic, have shade coverage on at least 40 percent of its land, and meet a minimum diversity quota for trees and flora—amongst other prerequisites. Farms also have to pay—not just for the SMBC certification, but also the initial organic one.

SHADE-GROWN

And then some roasters also just label their coffee "shade-grown" without any specific certification. If you see it but aren't convinced, just call them up or visit the actual business and *ask* what exactly they mean by the term and how they can back up their claims. This is the cool thing about dealing with smaller-scale roasters instead of giant, faceless corporate behemoths—they're likely more than happy to talk about this stuff with you.

RAINFOREST ALLIANCE

An international nonprofit, the Rainforest Alliance's farm certification tends to get lumped in under the "environmental" banner (probably because its logo is a green frog and it sounds like the name of a hippie jam band), but in addition to things like not using certain pesticides and protecting wildlife, its list of ninety-nine criteria also includes many social and economic requirements, like safety standards, no child labor, and access to medical services. The farms don't have to meet *all* of the criteria (80 percent, with the exception of fifteen that are mandatory), so it is sometimes criticized for not being as strict and comprehensive as fair trade or other environmental certifications. If a coffee package has the Rainforest Alliance seal on it with no other qualifying text, then at least 90 percent of the beans inside should be certified. However, the package can contain as little as 30 percent so long as there is a written disclaimer. This certification also costs the farms to obtain.

Now what?

So you've found your perfect coffee retailer. You've found your perfect organic shade-grown direct-trade single-origin beans. You're home free, right? Nope. There are some things you as the consumer have to do to make sure your awesome coffee beans stay that way.

BUY SMALL

This should just be common sense: you know you need to use your coffee within a few weeks of roasting, and you don't want to waste any, so you should just buy the minimum amount available. But this is easier said than done, especially if you hate shopping or love buying in bulk. Again, try to re-conceptualize coffee as a perishable produce. You don't bulk-buy bananas or milk, and you're paying a hell of a lot more for beans than fruit or dairy.

You might also have to make some tough decisions. Say you only drink a cup or two a day, but the smallest bag your favorite roaster sells is 1 pound. Do you want to risk throwing out good coffee? Or keep drinking shitty coffee once it's past its prime? Or maybe you want to switch to your second-favorite roaster who sells 8-ounce bags?

STORE IT RIGHT

You're almost home free now, but there is still one more way you can screw up those beans, and that is by storing them incorrectly. Like, say, by putting them in your freezer or fridge. The only thing this will do is make your coffee taste like frozen peas and old mayonnaise. Leaving a bag of beans open on your counter is another way to ruin them—exposure to oxygen, sunlight, heat, and moisture will quickly make the coffee go bad (not to mention ants and mice and whatever other gross stuff you have living in your kitchen).

And for the love of god, don't store your beans in your coffee grinder. Cafés can fill their hoppers (those are the plastic thingies on top of the machines that hold the beans before grinding) with beans because they go through so many, so quickly. You're going to be making a few cups a day. Measure out how many beans you actually need for each brew, and only put that amount in there.

The right place to store your beans is somewhere cool, dark, and dry, and in an airtight container—ideally plastic or glass, because tins can make the coffee taste metallic.

Further Reading

> If you want to understand more about sustainable coffee and the impact your caffeine habit has on the rest of the world, *The Coffee Book: Anatomy of an Industry from Crop to the Last Drop* by Nina Luttinger and Gregory Dicum is a good primer. One of the authors used to work for the predecessor to Fair Trade USA, so the book leans heavily in that direction,

and it is a little out of date. But its explorations of the economic, social, political, and environmental ramifications of the global coffee trade are still totally relevant, and it's full of fascinating facts and figures about the market.

SEVEN

Recipes

So the moment of truth has arrived. You've found the perfect brewer and grinder for your taste and budget. You've brought home a 12-ounce bag of single-origin beans (roasted two days ago) from your favorite coffee shop. You've "borrowed" a food scale and a thermometer from your parents' kitchen. You cleaned that novelty coffee mug you got as your workplace Secret Santa gift. You have everything you need to start creating amazing coffee at home. Now you just need to work out how.

The following recipes are by no means the final word on making coffee, but they are a first word. Before you get started, here are a few more pieces of advice:

Ratio Profiling Is Encouraged

This may sound crazy, but the least important information in these recipes is the measurements. Most brewers do not have one specific "right" amount of coffee or water to use. If you polled fifty good baristas on how they prepare coffee in a Chemex, each would give a different amount of coffee and water, and each would still be able to make a lovely cup with it.

As a general rule of thumb, a 1:16 coffee-to-water ratio is considered a good starting point for most methods, and most of the recipes in this book are around that figure. Testing out other ratios is not only fine, it's totally encouraged. The important thing is to be precise and methodical. Want something a little stronger? Don't just spoon in more coffee—measure out a 1:15 ratio. If you like that more, you will know exactly how to repeat it next time.

If this all sounds way too much like hard work, there is a very helpful online ratio convertor at *www.chriscorwin.com/coffee-water-ratio-calculator.*

Cool it

Never make your coffee with boiling water—the water you use should be between 195°F and 205°F. Either let the water sit for a minute, or use a thermometer.

Time is Not on Your Side

You know how you always think, "I'll just play this video game/read this book/trawl this Reddit thread/stay in this shower for five more minutes . . ." and then suddenly half an hour has passed? Your sense of time sucks. Use a timer when making any recipe that prescribes a specific length of time. You don't have to buy one, just find an app for your phone—preferably one that counts both up and down, and has an alarm.

Scale Up

As outlined in Chapter 5, your results will be way, way better if you measure both your coffee and water out by scale, instead of in spoons and cups. In most cases, you can just put your brewing device on the scale and press "tare," which will reset it to zero. Add the specified amount of coffee, press "tare" again, then slowly add the water until you hit the desired amount.

Also, to keep in line with the standard terminology in the coffee industry—and because it's much easier to weigh out—these recipes use grams instead of ounces. Don't blame me, blame Ronald Reagan for ending America's metrication efforts. This book includes a conversation chart in Appendix B and there are plenty of apps and websites that can convert figures from or to imperial and metric measurements. Most scales will also have settings for both.

Grind First, Grind Right

None of these recipes include grinding the beans as a step because you are an intelligent person who doesn't need to be told that your beans need to be ground before brewing. Grind your coffee before doing anything else (except maybe putting the kettle on; that's okay), but not too far before—you want it to be as freshly ground as possible.

The grind levels in these recipes are described in terms like fine, medium, coarse, and variations thereof, which is pretty meaningless if you have no frame of reference. Here is a rough guide to what those should look like:

- ⟩ Very fine: flour
- ⟩ Fine: table salt
- ⟩ Medium: sand
- ⟩ Coarse: kosher salt.

Don't Half-Ass It—Yet

We both know you're not going to follow these recipes to the letter every single time. Sometimes you will eyeball things instead of weighing them. Sometimes you will use pre-ground coffee. Sometimes you will pour the whole drink straight from the brewer into your mouth because you're running late for work and have no clean cups. But it's good to have done things by the book at least a few times so you know what you're sacrificing when you inevitably half-ass it.

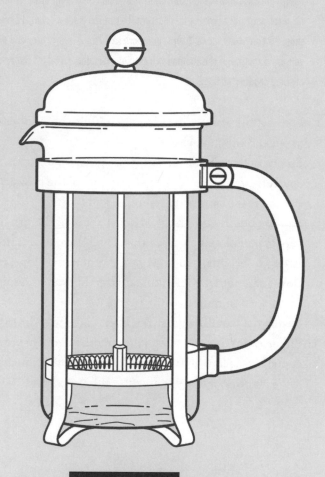

A French press.

French Press

French presses come in many different sizes, and the amount of water and coffee you will need for each will of course be different. This recipe is for a small, 12-ounce press (which should theoretically make 3 cups, but more like 2 cups in practice, and more like 1 cup if you use a mug), but this method is incredibly versatile, so adjust the ratios for taste and brewing capacity as needed.

1. Pre-heat the French press by filling it with boiling water while you grind and weigh your coffee.
2. Empty out the water used for pre-heating, and put 20 grams of coarsely ground coffee into the bottom of the brewer.
3. Put the French press on the scale, and hit "tare."
4. Slowly pour in 300 grams of hot water over the grounds, making sure to completely saturate them, and leave to sit uncovered.
5. After 30 seconds, give the layer of grounds on top a gentle stir.
6. Cover the pot with the lid and filter, but don't plunge down yet. Leave for 4 minutes.
7. Firmly but carefully press the filter all the way down.
8. Either pour the *entire* contents of the French press into your cup(s), or decant into a thermos or carafe immediately—if you leave it sitting in the pot, it will continue to brew.

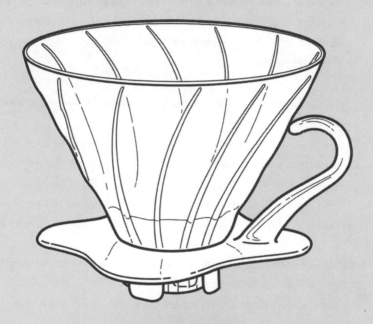

The Hario V60.

Hario V60

One of the most popular pour-over brewers, the V60 is also one of the trickiest to master. It has a much larger hole at its base compared to other similar brewers, so the liquid drips through really fast and it can be difficult to stay in control. Hario sells its own filters for the V60 and you will need to get your hands on some—regular filters are the wrong shape. This recipe is for the 02 model V60, which is the most common one you will find in the United States, though the company does make larger and smaller versions, so double check which you have.

1. While heating your water, put the V60 on top of a cup or carafe, and open a paper filter inside.
2. Once the water is boiled, pour it over the filter until it is totally wet, then discard any of the excess water from the cup. Put the whole setup on your scale.
3. Put 21 grams of fine- to medium-ground coffee in the filter, and make sure it is sitting evenly. Hit "tare" on your scale, and start your timer.
4. Slowly pour just enough hot water into the center of the grounds to fully saturate them, then gently stir. Wait 30 seconds.
5. Slowly start pouring again, moving in a clockwise circle. Again, do not pour onto the filter. Try to keep the water level consistent. Stop pouring when the scale reads 315 grams. This should be about the 3-minute mark.
6. Wait until the liquid slows to a drip, and remove the V60.

The Kalita Wave.

Kalita Wave

If the V60 was the iPod of pour-overs—the stylish phenom that made a dorky name cool again—the Kalita Wave is the iPhone—better looking, easier to use, more expensive, and Oh So Hot Right Now. The major features that make this brewer stand apart are a flat bottom (with three small holes in it) and the wavy custom paper filters, both of which make it easier to get a very even extraction. This recipe is for the single-serve 155 model. There is also a larger model called the 185.

1. While heating your water, put the Wave on top of a cup or carafe, and put a paper filter inside.
2. Dampen the filter by pouring hot water down into the exact center. *Do not* pour directly onto the sides, or the filter will droop like a depressed basset hound. Discard any excess water in the cup, and place the whole setup on your scale.
3. Put in 22 grams of medium-ground coffee. "Tare" the scale, and start your timer.
4. Slowly pour in enough hot water to saturate the grounds, and leave for 30 seconds.
5. Start slowly pouring in more water, moving in clockwise circles. When the water level gets close to the top, stop pouring and wait until it is about halfway down the filter again. Repeat until the scale says 360 grams. The timer should be around 3 to 3½ minutes.
6. Wait until the liquid stops dripping, and remove the Wave.

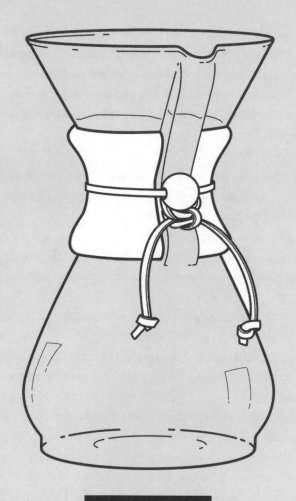

A Chemex brewer.

Chemex

This recipe is for a 30-ounce, 6-cup Chemex, but the iconic glass brewer comes in several other sizes. For no very good reason that I can tell, Chemex makes several different filter shapes—square, half-circle, and half-moon—and they come in folded and unfolded versions. Buy the folded versions (I'm all for manual coffee making, but come on). Also note that the 3-cup Chemex uses a slightly different filter, and won't work with those made for larger models.

1. While heating the water, unfold the filter into a conical shape, with 3 sheets on one side, and 1 sheet on the other. Put it into the Chemex with the 3-sheet side against the spout.

2. Wet the entire filter (or as much as you can manage if you're using the square filter; the corners sticking up out the top don't matter that much) with hot water, then pour the water back out of the Chemex.

3. Put 50 grams of medium- to coarse-ground coffee in the filter. Put the Chemex onto your scale, and hit "tare." Start your timer.

4. Slowly pour in enough hot water to saturate the grounds, moving in clockwise circles. Don't pour water directly onto the side of the filter.

5. Let the coffee rest for 45 seconds, then start pouring again with the same motion. Try to keep the water level steady, about halfway down the filter. Stop pouring when the scale is at 750 grams. The timer should be around 4 minutes.

6. When the stream has slowed to a staggered drip, take out the filter.

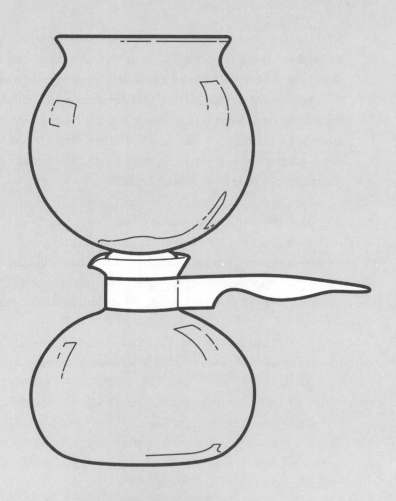

A siphon or vac pot.

Siphon

Siphon brewers, or vacuum pots, come in all sorts of shapes, filter types, and price ranges, but they all work basically the same way. As a result, this recipe is a bit of a one-size-fits-all and I have tried to account for several different variations you might find in brewers. Still, if you come across something and think, "Mine does *not* do that," refer to the instructions that came with the brewer, or consult your old pal Google. One thing this recipe can't account for is brewer size—the measurements here are for a 20-ounce or 5-cup brewer, because most brands offer one of those. The ratio I'm using is 1:15, so adjust measurements accordingly if you're using a different sized model.

1. Boil water in a kettle. Many people heat the water all the way in the siphon itself, but it's so much quicker to pre-boil.
2. Fit your filter into the upper chamber. Cloth filters will need to be rinsed first for about a minute, while paper filters just need to be wet until they are soaked through. Metal filters can slot straight in.
3. Pour 600 grams of boiling water into the lower chamber, and place that over your heat source. If this is a stovetop model, then it just sits on your stove. Otherwise, attach it to whatever stand it came with, and light the burner underneath. If you are able to, loosely place the upper chamber on top while it heats, but don't seal it in.
4. Just when the water in the lower chamber is about to boil, seal the upper chamber in place. Marvel as the water rises up into the top chamber. (You're a wizard, Harry!)
5. When the water in the upper chamber reaches 200°F, add 40 grams of ground coffee. Siphon brewers work with a variety of grind sizes—start with a medium grind, then try different levels of coarseness until you hit on one you like.

6. Gently and briefly stir the coffee to ensure all the grounds are wet. Turn down the heat a little. Wait 45 seconds, and stir again.

7. After another 45 seconds, remove the brewer from its heat source. This will mean either taking it off the stove or moving the whole apparatus away from the burner, or moving the burner itself away. Gloves are not a terrible idea for this task.

8. Stir the coffee gently and briefly again, using a circular motion.

9. As it cools, the liquid will sink back down into the lower chamber, leaving the grounds up at the top.

10. When the liquid has finished draining, remove the upper chamber. You can pour straight from the lower chamber into a cup.

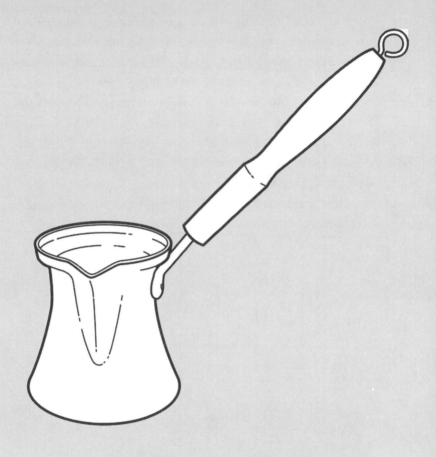

An ibrik, used to make Turkish coffee.

Turkish

The toughest part about making Turkish coffee well may be grinding the coffee down fine enough. The coffee for this method needs to be ground even finer than for espresso, so you will need either a good-quality electric burr grinder, or a specialty Turkish hand-grinder to pull it off. You want the final product to be very thick and strong, so the ratios here are smaller (basically, you will put in less water for every gram of coffee) than other brewing methods. This recipe is for a 10-ounce ibrik, which should make 3 to 4 little cups. Speaking of, you really can't drink this stuff out of a regular mug, or you'll end up with a mouthful of grounds. If you don't have any of those really pretty specialty Turkish cups, a regular demitasse should suffice. If you don't have a demitasse . . . try a shot glass.

1. Pour 220 grams of cold water into the pot, then add 20 grams of very finely ground coffee and give it a good stir.
2. If you want to add sugar or spices, do this now. You really don't want to add these things after brewing because you don't want to stir up the sediment in your cup. Measurements here are kind of a personal preference, but try a teaspoon of sugar on your first attempt, then adjust subsequent brews to taste.
3. Put the pot on the stove, and turn it on to a low heat.
4. When the brew starts to foam and is just near boiling—but, crucially, not actually boiling—take the pot off the heat.
5. Give it about 20 seconds to settle back down, then put it back on the heat.
6. Bring it back up to a near boil again, and repeat the process.
7. Choose your own adventure: If you want to get the coffee even frothier, you can repeat the process a third time. If not, go to Step 8.
8. Let the coffee cool and settle for a few seconds. Carefully pour into cups, making sure each gets an equal amount of froth.

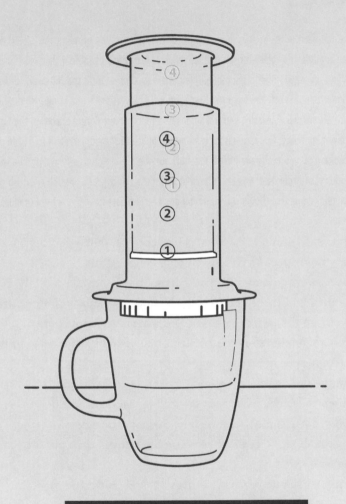

Regular brewing with the AeroPress.

AeroPress

The AeroPress is a surprisingly flexible brewer—you can experiment widely with different grind sizes, ratios, filters, and steep times and still get great results. This recipe is your straightforward, meat-and-potatoes method—not so different from the one that comes in the box (but still different, because that one is not great). If you want something a bit less conventional, check out the proceeding recipe.

1. While boiling water, put a paper filter in the black cap and rinse with water until it is fully soaked (some prefer to use hot water for this so the filter will preheat the brewer; you can do that if you're so inclined).

2. Screw the cap onto the larger cylinder, and put it on top of your cup (or carafe) with the cap at the bottom. Place the whole setup on your scale.

3. Add 17 grams of fine- to medium-ground coffee. "Tare" the scale.

4. Pour in 250 grams of water.

5. Stir (the AeroPress comes with its own stirring stick, but you can use anything) and let it sit for 30 seconds.

6. Insert the smaller cylinder and plunge down firmly and evenly, but not too quickly, until you hear the hiss of air escaping. This should take about 30 to 45 seconds.

7. You can either drink the brew as is, or dilute it with some water to taste.

8. **Bonus step:** To clean, just screw the cap off, hold the AeroPress over a trashcan, and push the plunger through as far as it will go. The entire coffee puck should fall out, leaving very little mess behind. This delightfully simple cleaning method will make your drink approximately 18 percent more enjoyable.

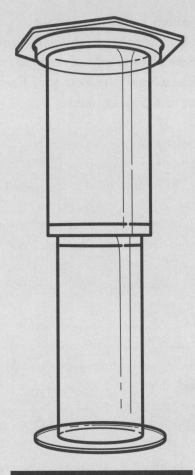

An inverted AeroPress.

Inverted AeroPress

The previous AeroPress method is similar to the one its creator recommends, but it is not similar to the way most coffee geeks actually use the device these days. More popular now is the "inverted" method, in which you basically flip the device upside down to allow the coffee to steep longer before plunging. This allows for a more even and controlled extraction, and is closer to other forms of immersion brewing, like the French press. On the downside, it is more involved, messier, and more time-consuming, and requires you to perform a slightly risky balancing act, pouring water into the brewer while it is standing on its smaller end on a scale.

1. While boiling water, put a paper filter in the black cap and rinse with water until it is fully soaked. You don't need it just yet, but you may as well get this out of the way first.
2. Insert the smaller cylinder into the larger one, so that the rubber is at the edge of the number four circle.
3. Flip the AeroPress so the smaller cylinder is at the bottom, and stand it on its end on top of your scale, with the opening facing the ceiling.
4. Add 17 grams of fine- to medium-ground coffee. Be very careful not to get any on the lip of the cylinder, or you will have trouble screwing the cap on. "Tare" your scale.
5. Pour in 250 grams of hot water and give the mixture a gentle stir.
6. Screw the cap and filter on the top, and leave to sit for 2 minutes.
7. Quickly flip the AeroPress over, placing the filter side down on top of a cup or carafe.
8. Plunge down firmly and evenly for 30 to 45 seconds until you can hear the hiss of air escaping, and remove the AeroPress.

The Clever Coffee Dripper.

Clever Coffee Dripper

The Clever comes in two sizes: the more common 18-ounce version, and a smaller 11-ounce model. This recipe is for the former. Both models use a number 4 paper filter, even though it's kind of an awkward fit in the smaller one (you just have to smoosh the lid down over the floppy wet paper).

1. While boiling your water, unfold the paper filter inside the brewer. Once the water is hot, wet the filter completely, and pour or drain the excess water out.
2. Put 20 grams of medium- to coarse-ground coffee in the bottom.
3. Pour 100 grams of hot water, fully saturating the grounds, and give it a gentle stir.
4. Add another 200 grams of hot water. Put the lid on, and let it steep for 3 ½ minutes.
5. Take off the lid and carefully place the Clever on top of a mug or carafe.
6. As the liquid starts to drain, give it a quick stir.
7. Once it has drained completely, lift the brewer off the cup (pro tip: put it down on the lid, in case any last drips escape).

A moka pot.

Moka Pot

This recipe doesn't really use precise measurements because the exact size of your moka pot is going to dictate how much coffee and water you use. Of course, to reduce wastage on future brews, you may want to note exactly how much that is. But hooray for not having to use a scale or a thermometer.

1. Pre-boil water in a kettle. This may seem unnecessary, but it is actually faster, and it will reduce the risk of the pot overheating and burning your coffee.
2. Meanwhile, fill the filter basket with finely ground coffee. Fill it all the way to the top, but do not push or tamp the coffee down—the water needs to be able to push through the grounds during brewing. Just brush any excess grounds off with your finger.
3. Once your water has boiled, fill the lower chamber of the pot up to the valve.
4. Put the filter basket into the lower chamber, and tightly screw the upper chamber on top.
5. Put the pot on your stove, over a medium heat. Leave the lid open so you can see the magic happen.
6. Watch the brew bubble into the upper chamber until you hear it sputter and see the water dry up, then remove it from the heat and close the lid.
7. Serve immediately.

The Eva Solo Café Solo.

Café Solo

This recipe is for the 1-liter Café Solo model, which may sound big, but is actually the company's midsize model. Clearly, this is a brewer made for sharing, though there's nothing stopping you halving the amount of coffee and water if you're drinking, err, solo.

1. Zip the Neoprene case over the brewer (seriously; you'll burn your hand if you don't), and preheat the glass carafe by filling it with boiling water while you grind and weigh your coffee.
2. Pour the water out and place the brewer on your scale. Put in 60 grams of coarsely ground coffee, and "tare" the scale.
3. Pour in 850 grams of hot water, and stir for 10 seconds.
4. Wait for 20 seconds, then insert the filter and lid in the top of the brewer, and let steep for another 3 ½ minutes.
5. Remove the lid, and either gently pour the entire contents into cups, or decant immediately into a thermos or carafe. Just don't leave the coffee sitting in the brewer.

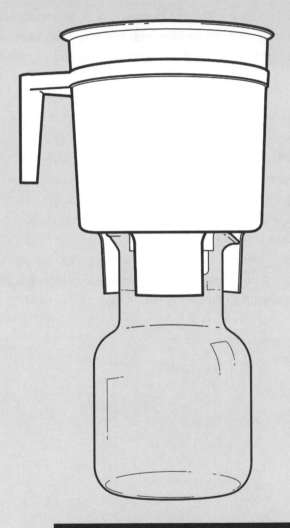

A Toddy Cold Brew Coffee Maker.

Cold Brew

The two main cold brew brewers are—to use their full titles—the Toddy Cold Brew Coffee Maker and the Filtron Cold Water Brewer. They're basically the same, so let's kill two birds with one stone with a guide that should work for both.

1. Place the rubber stopper in the underside of the brewer.
2. Dampen the filter pad with cold water, and place it in the cavity in the bottom of the inside of the brewer.
3. **Optional step:** the Filtron also comes with paper liners; you don't really need them, but they make cleaning easier, and will reduce wear on the filter pads. If you want to use one, unfold it inside the brewer now.
4. Add in 454 grams (that's a whole pound) of coarsely ground coffee.
5. **Another optional step:** The Filtron comes with a plastic cover it calls a "grounds guard" and a second plastic chamber. You are supposed to put these on top of the main chamber now, but put them in after adding water if you prefer to have more control over the contact between the water and grounds.
6. Gently pour in 2,000 grams (that's 2 liters) of cold water, working in a circular motion and submerging all of the grounds. If some of the grounds at the top still look dry, you can very gently push them down with a spoon, but don't stir.
7. If you are using the Filtron and haven't put the grounds guard and top chamber on yet, do it now. If you are using the Toddy and have a gross kitchen with flies and dust, or roommates you don't trust, you can cover the top of the brewer with plastic wrap, foil, or a plate.
8. Let the brew steep for 12 hours.

9. Remove the rubber stopper from the bottom of the brewer and quickly place it on top of the decanter. This is far easier with a second person. Leave to drain (this could take a while).

10. Remove the brewer, put a lid on top of the decanter, and refrigerate.

11. The concentrate will keep for a week or two (assuming it lasts that long). To serve, pour it into a glass (with or without ice) and add water to taste (one part concentrate to three parts water is standard, but use whatever tastes best to you).

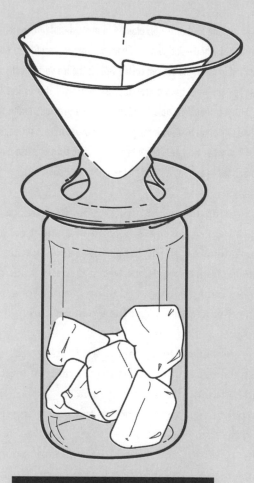

A pour-over brewed over ice
to create iced coffee.

Hot-Brewed Iced Coffee

This way of making iced coffee (explained in more detail in Chapter 4) can be done with any pour-over method—including a Chemex—or an AeroPress. But it should be done with a method in which the brewed coffee will hit the ice very shortly after its contact with hot water. You can't just brew a French press then pour it over ice. This recipe is for the Chemex, but you should be able to adapt both the previous Kalita Wave and Hario V60 recipes (and any other pour-over recipe), or either AeroPress recipe, by replacing half the amount of hot water with ice. For all of those, make sure you use a mug or carafe that is large enough to hold all the ice *and* all the incoming liquid.

1. While heating the water, unfold the filter into a conical shape, with three sheets on one side, and one sheet on the other. Put it into the Chemex with the three-sheet side against the spout.
2. Wet the entire filter with hot water. Usually, taking wet filters out of brewers before you've used them is a bad idea, but in this case, you'll have to in order to get the ice in. So *carefully* remove the filter, and pour out any water.
3. Put the Chemex on your scale and add in 375 grams of ice cubes.
4. Replace the paper filter, and add 50 grams of medium- to coarse-ground coffee inside. "Tare" your scale.
5. Slowly pour in 50 grams of hot water, saturating the grounds and moving in clockwise circles.
6. Let the coffee rest for 45 seconds, then start pouring again with the same motion. Stop pouring when the scale is at 375 grams.
7. When the stream has slowed to a staggered drip, take the filter out and pour into a glass. Stir before drinking.

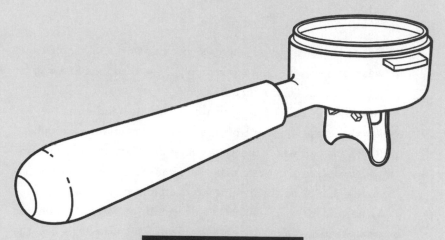

An espresso portafilter.

Espresso

So you totally ignored my advice and went and bought an espresso machine anyway, huh? Or someone gave you one for your birthday? Or you just want to know how espresso should be made in theory? Fine. Just understand that it is much tougher than brewing a French press. There are entire books dedicated solely to making espresso. With that in mind, here is a rough guide that should at least help make your early attempts suck a bit less.

1. Depending on how your espresso machine works, either fill it with water or connect it to a water supply. Then turn it on and wait for it to warm up. This could take a while.
2. Take the portafilter (that's the thing with the handle and the basket the coffee goes in) off the espresso machine's grouphead (that's the part where the water comes out). If your machine came with two sizes of baskets, make sure it is the larger one, which is a double. If it is the smaller one, pry it off and switch them.
3. Wipe and dry the basket, while running water through the grouphead to make sure both are clean. This also helps heat the grouphead if your machine has been running a while.
4. Finely grind between 19 and 21 grams of coffee into the basket. Swipe any excess off the top with your finger.
5. Place a tamper (that's the circular thing that looks a bit like a doorknob) on top of the coffee and press down firmly. Take the tamper off and make sure the coffee bed is flat and even (hint: it is easier to achieve this if you tamp while resting the portafilter on a flat surface). Swipe the rim of the basket with your finger again to make sure it's clean.
6. Very carefully put the portafilter back in the grouphead. Place a demitasse underneath.

7. Start the extraction (there will be a switch of some kind to turn on) and turn off when the brown stream turns golden. This should take about 25 to 30 seconds, and should yield about 1 ½ to 2 ounces of espresso. If this is way off, try adjusting your grind next time.

8. Drink your espresso straight, or use it in conjunction with steamed milk, as outlined in the next recipe.

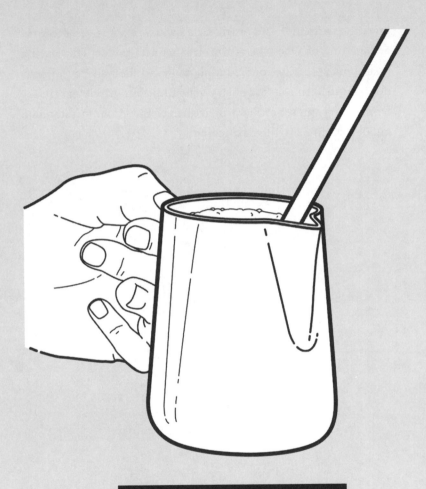

Steaming milk for espresso drinks.

Milk for Espresso Drinks

Once you have nailed the previous recipe for espresso (or perhaps if you haven't and want to compensate by drowning your crappy shots in milk), you can begin learning to make other espresso drinks (if not for yourself, then for your family and friends, who *will* demand free lattes). When starting out, it is a good idea to put a thermometer in your pitcher—you want a metal one with a clip to hold it in place, which you can get for about $10. It is also a good idea to stock up on way more milk than you think you need—you're going to screw this up many times before you get it right.

1. Both your milk and milk pitcher need to be cold. Both should be stored in the fridge.
2. Pour milk into your pitcher, stopping when it's just under the beginning of where the spout protrudes from the rest of the jug.
3. Turn on the steamer for a few seconds to purge any water, then move the steaming wand out from the machine.
4. Position the tip of the steaming wand about half an inch under the surface level of the milk. Don't let the tip touch the side of the pitcher.
5. Turn on the steam, then grip the pitcher so your nondominant hand is holding the handle and your dominant hand is cupping the side. This is necessary both so you can feel the temperature of the pitcher as it heats, and also so your dominant hand is free to quickly turn off the steam if and when needed.
6. When you can feel a bit of heat coming through the pitcher, submerge the wand deeper into the milk, being careful not to touch the bottom or side. The milk should start moving in a whirlpool.
7. If you are using a thermometer, wait until the temperature is at about 150 degrees. If you aren't, wait until the pitcher is too hot to keep your hand on it.

8. Turn off steam, then lower the pitcher off the wand. Do it in this order, or things will get messy.

9. Wipe the wand immediately with a clean cloth. You'll thank me next time you go to use it.

10. Tap the bottom of the pitcher against a table or bench a couple times to pop any large bubbles, then swirl the contents around a few times to better integrate the foam and milk.

11. Exactly how you pour the milk into your espresso will depend on what kind of drink you're making, but as a general rule: start with a bit of height, pouring into the center of the cup, moving the pitcher down closer to the coffee as you go. Once you get the hang of it, you can start playing around with latte art.

Further Reading

> Brew Methods (*www.brewmethods.com*) is a great repository of links to written and video brew guides by top roasters and baristas.

> Most of the big-name (and plenty of the lesser-known) third-wave roasters have brew guides for several different devices (typically the ones they sell) on their websites, often with photos or videos.

> If you want to get deeper into the scientific side of coffee-making, *The Professional Barista's Handbook: An Expert's Guide to Preparing Espresso, Coffee, and Tea* and *Everything But Espresso* by Scott Rao (*www.scottrao.com*) are very highly regarded in the industry, and mix practical, illustrated step-by-step instructions with serious data and impressive-looking graphs.

> *How to Make Coffee Before You've Had Coffee: Ristretto Roasters' Spectacularly Simple Guide to Brewing at Home* is a great little no-bullshit recipe book written by the owner of Ristretto Roasters in Portland, Oregon. The Kindle version is an insane bargain—it costs less than a cappuccino plus tip.

Glossary

ACIDITY
Unlike stomach acid or battery acid, acidity in coffee is a good thing. It refers to an enjoyable brightness or liveliness, similar to biting into a tart green apple.

BARISTA
A person who makes coffee by day, plays in a band/draws indie comics/performs standup comedy/dreams of Hollywood stardom by night.

BATCH BREWING
Once called "making coffee" in a coffee shop, this process involves brewing a large amount of coffee—whether in a machine or a large French press—to be poured to order, as opposed to brewing individual cups to order. If you go into most coffee shops and simply ask for "coffee," this is still what you will likely be served.

BODY
A way to describe how dense the coffee feels in your mouth. For comparison, Guinness has a full or heavy body and Bud has a light body.

BLOOM
Pouring a small amount of hot water onto coffee to release the gases trapped inside before brewing. Basically, making the coffee fart. This makes extraction easier.

CHICORY
A woody plant historically used as a filler or replacement in coffee during shortages or tough economic times. Still commonly consumed by drunk tourists in New Orleans.

COFFEE BAR
A more pretentious name for a café, which is a more pretentious name for a coffee shop.

CREMA
The lighter brown foam that appears on the top of espresso. Or should, anyway—crema's presence (or rather a lack there of) is the quickest way to tell whether a shot of espresso sucks. Which is not to say that espresso with good crema can't still suck.

DECAF
Coffee without meaning.

EXTRACTION
The process by which water steals all of the delicious flavors from the coffee grounds. If coffee is under-extracted (often because it is ground too coarsely, the water is too cold, or the brewing time is too short), it will taste weak and watery. If it is over-extracted (ground too fine, water too hot, or brewed too long), it will also pick up too many of the not-so-delicious flavors from the beans or taste burnt.

GREEN BEANS
Unroasted coffee beans, not the thing your mom puts in a casserole at Thanksgiving.

JAVA
Refers either to an island in Indonesia where coffee is grown, or just a general synonym for "coffee," but never the programming language.

LATTE ART
The fancy designs and images baristas pour into your espresso drinks. Don't read anything into receiving a cappuccino with a heart on top— it's just the easiest thing to make.

MOUTHFEEL
Literally how the coffee feels in your mouth—oily, milky, astringent, or buttery, for instance.

NANO-ROASTER
The term "micro-roaster" can refer to anything from some dude who roasts 20 pounds a week in his garage to a business supplying beans to cafés and restaurants all across a city. "Nano-roaster" is even less specific—there is literally no actual definition—but is generally agreed to be more specifically that dude in his garage.

PULL
In coffee lingo, an espresso shot is "pulled." This dates back to when espresso machines had actual levers on them. Now they have buttons, but "switching on an espresso shot" doesn't have quite the same ring to it.

SOURNESS

Instead of acidity, which is a positive feature, its ugly cousin sourness is an unwelcome presence in coffee. Unlike apple or grapefruit, this is more like vinegar or medicine.

SPICY

Describing a coffee as "spicy" means you can taste spices—like cinnamon, ginger, or cardamom—not that it's burning your mouth like a curry or a forkful of kimchi.

TAMPER

A circular press used to compress grounds into an espresso filter basket. Also known as a really expensive hunk of metal and wood (high-end models get into the hundreds of dollars).

U.S./Metric Measurements Conversion Charts

VOLUME CONVERSIONS	
U.S. VOLUME MEASURE	METRIC EQUIVALENT
⅛ teaspoon	0.5 milliliter
¼ teaspoon	1 milliliter
½ teaspoon	2 milliliters
1 teaspoon	5 milliliters
½ tablespoon	7 milliliters
1 tablespoon (3 teaspoons)	15 milliliters
2 tablespoons (1 fluid ounce)	30 milliliters
¼ cup (4 tablespoons)	60 milliliters
⅓ cup	90 milliliters
½ cup (4 fluid ounces)	125 milliliters
⅔ cup	160 milliliters
¾ cup (6 fluid ounces)	180 milliliters
1 cup (16 tablespoons)	250 milliliters
1 pint (2 cups)	500 milliliters
1 quart (4 cups)	1 liter (about)

WEIGHT CONVERSIONS	
U.S. WEIGHT MEASURE	METRIC EQUIVALENT
½ ounce	15 grams
1 ounce	30 grams
2 ounces	60 grams
3 ounces	85 grams
¼ pound (4 ounces)	115 grams
½ pound (8 ounces)	225 grams
¾ pound (12 ounces)	340 grams
1 pound (16 ounces)	454 grams

OVEN TEMPERATURE CONVERSIONS	
DEGREES FAHRENHEIT	DEGREES CELSIUS
200 degrees F	95 degrees C
250 degrees F	120 degrees C
275 degrees F	135 degrees C
300 degrees F	150 degrees C
325 degrees F	160 degrees C
350 degrees F	180 degrees C
375 degrees F	190 degrees C
400 degrees F	205 degrees C
425 degrees F	220 degrees C
450 degrees F	230 degrees C

BAKING PAN SIZES	
AMERICAN	METRIC
8 × 1½ inch round baking pan	20 × 4 cm cake tin
9 × 1½ inch round baking pan	23 × 3.5 cm cake tin
11 × 7 × 1½ inch baking pan	28 × 18 × 4 cm baking tin
13 × 9 × 2 inch baking pan	30 × 20 × 5 cm baking tin
2 quart rectangular baking dish	30 × 20 × 3 cm baking tin
15 × 10 × 2 inch baking pan	30 × 25 × 2 cm baking tin (Swiss roll tin)
9 inch pie plate	22 × 4 or 23 × 4 cm pie plate
7 or 8 inch springform pan	18 or 20 cm springform or loose-bottom cake tin
9 × 5 × 3 inch loaf pan	23 × 13 × 7 cm or 2 lb narrow loaf or pâté tin
1½ quart casserole	1.5 liter casserole
2 quart casserole	2 liter casserole

Index

About the Author

RUTH BROWN is an Australian-born journalist and writer. She currently works as the arts and entertainment editor at the *Brooklyn Paper*, and previously worked as an editor and reporter at *Willamette Week* in Portland, Oregon—the best coffee city in the country (yeah, you heard me, San Francisco). When not imbibing medically inadvisable amounts of caffeine, she enjoys combat sports and pub rock.